American Law

To Madeline, Eloise, and Christine

American Law
A Comparative Primer

GERRIT DE GEEST

Charles F. Nagel Professor of International and Comparative Law, Washington University School of Law, USA

Edward Elgar
PUBLISHING

Cheltenham, UK • Northampton, MA, USA

Published by
Edward Elgar Publishing Limited
The Lypiatts
15 Lansdown Road
Cheltenham
Glos GL50 2JA
UK

Edward Elgar Publishing, Inc.
William Pratt House
9 Dewey Court
Northampton
Massachusetts 01060
USA

A catalogue record for this book
is available from the British Library

Library of Congress Control Number: 2020939124

ISBN 978 1 83910 144 1 (cased)
ISBN 978 1 83910 145 8 (eBook)
ISBN 978 1 83910 146 5 (paperback)

Printed and bound in Great Britain by TJ International Ltd, Padstow, Cornwall

Contents

About the author

Gerrit De Geest is the Charles F. Nagel Professor of International and Comparative Law at Washington University School of Law, where he teaches comparative law, contracts, law and economics, and served as the director of the Center on Law, Innovation & Economic Growth. Before moving to St. Louis with his family, he was a chaired professor at the Utrecht School of Economics and president of the European Association of Law and Economics. He is author of *Rents: How Marketing Causes Inequality* (Beccaria Books, 2018), and editor of *Economics of Comparative Law* (Edward Elgar, 2009), *Comparative Law and Economics* (Edward Elgar, 2004, 3 volumes, with R. Van den Bergh) and the *Encyclopedia of Law and Economics* (Edward Elgar, 2000, 5 volumes, with B. Bouckaert).

Acknowledgements

The insights on which this book is based have been shaped by countless discussions with colleagues. I thank Adam Badawi, Scott Baker, Boudewijn Bouckaert, Kevin Collins, Robert Cooter, Peter Cramer, Giuseppe Dari-Mattiacci, Jef De Mot, Ben Depoorter, Danielle D'Onfro, John Drobak, Dan Epps, Nuno Garoupa, Tom Ginsburg, Ton Hol, Ewoud Hondius, Mitja Kovac, Saul Levmore, Francesco Parisi, Adam Rosenzweig, Hans-Bernd Schaefer, Brian Tamanaha, Andrew Tuch, Tom Ulen and Roger Van den Bergh for insightful comments on parts of the project. I have also benefited from comments made by students in my Comparative Law course. A special thanks goes to John Haley, who made me realize how crucial geography, history, and culture are to the understanding of legal differences.

I developed some of the insights in two articles: Gerrit De Geest, "Understanding French, German, and Civil Law More Generally" in Jef De Mot (ed), *Liber amicorum Boudewijn Bouckaert. Vrank en vrij* (Brugge, die Keure, 2012) 3–16 and Gerrit De Geest, "Old Law Is Cheap Law" in Michael Faure, Wicher Schreuders and Louis Visscher (eds), *Don't Take It Seriously: Essays in Law and Economics in Honour of Roger Van den Bergh* (Cambridge, Intersentia, 2018) 505–23.

I thank my research assistant Shin-Ru Cheng for insightful comments. I have received research support from Washington University School of Law.

Finally, I am grateful to my wife, Christine Vandenabeele, for our numerous conversations about cultural differences. These have shaped my thinking more than all those thick books I have read.

Preface

If you are an international student and you study American law, you are puzzled for two different reasons. First, you are puzzled because 90% of American law turns out to be the same as the law in your country. Secondly, you are puzzled because you don't understand why those 10% differences exist. There seems to be no deeper explanation—differences among legal systems seem to exist randomly. Similarly, if you grew up in the U.S. and study American law, you may have a hard time identifying what is typical for American law. You may also feel that some rules make more sense than others, but you have a hard time pointing out what exactly bothers you about certain rules, especially because you don't know the alternatives. If the books you are studying only deal with American law, they don't make you analyse what is typically American about certain rules. This is like studying your dog without having seen a different animal in your life—it would be hard to say what is typical for a dog. You may think that all animals bark or slide over a carpet trying to catch a ball. But believe me, a cow will never slide over your carpet trying to catch a ball the way your French bulldog does.

Most primers summarize American law irrespective of whether the law is different or the same in other countries. They neither explain the cultural nor the historical roots of the differences. If international students want to understand the cultural differences, they first need to understand what is typical about their own culture and their own legal system.

This primer wants to fill that gap. It is, in essence, a comparative law book in which American law receives 60% of the attention.

This book has three parts. The first part focuses on the core characteristic of American law—that it is largely judge-made law. It states in what fields the law is judge-made, and how common law countries differ from civil law countries. It also focuses on the role juries play, and on the fact that most law is state law—it differs from state to state. It gives guidance on how to read a court opinion, how to prepare for class, and how to prepare for exams at an American law school.

The second part of this book analyses American legal culture. It starts with a theory of why the English and French legal system started to diverge in late medieval times, with England developing a bottom-up system and France a top-down system. It then explains the cultural distinctions between universalism and particularism and between the notion of a corporation-as-a-family versus a corporation-as-a-project. It explains why civil law systems are more formalistic than common law systems, and why argumentation is less open in civil law systems. It discusses the legal realism movement in the U.S., and the relationship between law, religion and ethics. Finally, it discusses Levmore's uniformity thesis, and the "old law is cheap law" principle.

The third and final part of this book summarizes the main differences on this planet concerning law. It discusses criminal law, criminal procedure, civil procedure, evidence, constitutional law, administrative law, antitrust law, contract law, tort law and environmental regulation, property law, intellectual property law, corporate law, bankruptcy law, labor and employment law and antitrust law.

The book concludes with a reflection on whether American law is the best law on the planet. I am not going to tell you my conclusion now—consider this a cliffhanger.

1. Introduction: common law versus civil law

The United States is a common law country. France, Germany, China, Taiwan, Japan, and the Latin American countries are civil law countries. The terms common and civil law, however, also have more narrow definitions, so let's explore these as well.

Common law versus civil law countries. The term "common law" is usually used in its broad sense to refer to a legal system that has developed from a tradition that started in medieval England. What countries are we talking about? England, the United States (U.S.) (at least in 49 of the 50 states—not in Louisiana), Australia, Canada (except for in Quebec), New Zealand, Cyprus, Israel, India, Pakistan, Bhutan, Nepal, Bangladesh, Uganda, Singapore, and Jamaica, to name a few.

The Islamic law tradition. What countries are civil law? If we only distinguish between common and civil law, then all countries that are not common law countries are civil law countries. However, if we define the civil law tradition slightly more narrowly as the tradition going back to Roman law, then Islamic law has to be considered a third, independently developed legal tradition to which Saudi Arabia, Iran, Libya, and some other countries belong. Note that although Islam is the most practiced religion in Egypt and Turkey, Egypt has been so strongly influenced by French law and Turkey by German, Swiss, French, and Italian law that Egypt and Turkey are best classified as civil law countries.

French versus German tradition of civil law. Most countries on this planet are civil law countries. They can be divided into two groups. First, there is the French group, which includes Spain, Belgium, Italy, all Latin American countries, and most African countries. Secondly, there is the German tradition to which belong Austria, the Netherlands (sometimes wrongly classified in the French family), Russia, Switzerland, Estonia,

Latvia, Croatia, Slovenia, Serbia, Greece, and their former colonies. In addition, the German tradition includes East Asian countries such as Japan, South Korea and Taiwan. China has taken over elements of both the German and French tradition. The Scandinavian countries (Sweden, Denmark, Norway) form their own family, but they are closer to German law than to French law and therefore are sometimes included in the German family. Within North America, the American state Louisiana and the Canadian province Quebec are civil law systems, built on the French tradition. (The other 49 states of the U.S. and the other provinces in Canada are common law.)

The U.S. is the archetypical common law country. What country is the archetypical common law country? Some may say England, because that's where the tradition started. There are several arguments, however, to consider the U.S. the poster child of a common law country.

First, a larger part of the law is judge-made than in England. Secondly, in American law reviews and other legal literature, most commentators are writing in the *legal realism tradition.* They ask, "what is the problem in society that the legal rule tries to fix? And what is the best way to achieve that result?"

Thirdly, it is generally agreed in the U.S. that judges make the law, and law-making is seen as an inherently political activity. Relatedly, the nomination process for federal judges, and especially justices at the United States Supreme Court, is an openly political process with the President and the majority in the Senate as ultimate decision makers. There is no illusion here that judges only "find" the "objective" legal answer. To the contrary, it is known that the justices' political views drive their decisions regarding issues such as gun rights or abortion rights.

Common law versus statute law. In the U.S., common law is also used in a narrower sense for law that is judge-made and not derived from statutes. For instance, regarding consumer contracts, the common law of contracts applies as well as the statutory provisions in consumer protection law.

Common law versus equity. In an even more narrow sense, common law refers to rules made in the tradition of the common law courts that started in the 11th century, while equity refers to the law made by the Court of Chancery in a tradition that started in the 17th century. The

English economy was developing fast in the 17th century, but common law courts did not adapt the law fast enough. Therefore, a second court system was installed, called *equity*. Equity literally means fairness but the rules created by the Court of Chancery were not more or less fair than common law rules—they were just created by a different institution. For instance, common law courts held that breach of contract could only lead to monetary damages, but the equity court decided that in exceptional cases, when damages were hard to prove and therefore likely inadequate, specific performance could be granted. Over time, the Chancery made many such exceptions.

Common law courts and equity courts merged in the 1870s and are now administered by the same courts. The distinction between the common law and equity tradition, however, remains relevant because the Chancery did not use juries but only professional judges. Therefore, there is no right to a jury trial for legal rules developed in the equity tradition. For instance, to obtain specific performance as a remedy for contract breach, there is no jury trial, because the rules on specific performance have been developed by equity courts.

Delaware Court of Chancery. A few American states still have separate courts for law and equity. The best-known equity court is the Delaware Court of Chancery, which decides most cases involving Delaware corporations. What is the relationship between corporations and equity? Well, the law of corporations developed out of the law of trusts, which in turn developed out of the equity rules regarding fiduciary duties. Fiduciary duties originated from the equity courts. That's a long line of causation, but the bottom line is that most American corporations are incorporated in Delaware and that most Delaware cases of corporation law are done in front of professional judges, not jury laymen.

Civil law: narrower definitions. The term "civil law" usually refers to countries with a legal system that primarily relies on statute law and builds further on the Roman law tradition. Yet, just like the term "common law", civil law has more narrow definitions as well. In Roman times, civil law (*ius civile*) referred to the law that applied to Roman citizens and the term *ius gentium* referred to the law that was applied to non-citizens. In modern times, civil law is sometimes used to refer to everything that is covered in the Civil Code of Napoleon, which includes contract, tort and property law, but not merchant law, private international law or public law.

Stare decisis versus nonbinding precedents. In most civil law countries (Brazil is one of the exceptions), all law is presumed to be statute law. Therefore, there is no such thing as a precedent, that is, a court decision that forms the law. As a result, courts do not make precedents, and even "interpretations" made by courts are not binding to other courts. In common law countries, in contrast, precedents officially exist. Lower courts are bound by precedents of higher courts. This principle is called *stare decisis* which is Latin and means "stay with what has been decided". Higher courts are not bound by their own precedents though. This makes sense because if higher courts could not overrule their own precedents, the law could not evolve, as each precedent would be frozen forever.

Independent judges versus employees of the king. In the common law tradition, judges are fully independent. In the civil law tradition, judges are no more than employees of the king. They are strictly monitored by higher courts, which are in turn monitored to a remarkable extent by the central government.

We will later go deeper into the implications, but here is an illustration of what it means for judges to be viewed as employees of the government by the following anecdote. I once was in a juvenile court in Belgium (a country with a legal system in the French tradition) and noticed that the old paint was peeling off the walls. When I asked why they didn't repaint it, the judge replied that expenditures like this had to be approved by the government in Brussels. So, courts don't even get the autonomy to decide on repainting the walls!

PART I

American case method

2. American law is largely judge-made law

In the U.S., many rules have been made by courts. This differs from most other countries on the planet, where in principle only the legislator can make the rules and courts can do no more than strictly apply these rules.

This is not to say that the entire body of American law is made by judges— it depends on the field. In contract, tort, property and corporate law, most of the rules are judge-made. In some other fields, like consumer or antitrust law, the fundamental principles are articulated in statute law, but the detailed rules are left to the courts so that in practice courts make 90% of the rules. In consumer protection law, for instance, the Federal Trade Commission (FTC) Act forbids "unfair or deceptive acts or practices" without describing what these acts and practices are. As a result, the thousands of pages that deal with what is deceptive or unfair have been written by courts. Formally, these detailed norms may be presented as mere "interpretations" of those few words in the FTC Act, but in reality, there is little difference with pure common law, see Section 5 of the Federal Trade Commission Act, codified at 15 U.S.C. §45(a): "(1) Unfair methods of competition in or affecting commerce, and unfair or deceptive acts or practices in or affecting commerce, are hereby declared unlawful".

The same holds for antitrust law, where the Sherman Act forbids "attempts to monopolize" without describing what the term means. Did Microsoft illegally attempt to monopolize by integrating its web browser into Windows operating software? The court decided that Microsoft violated section 2 of the Sherman Act by employing anticompetitive means to maintain its monopoly power in the operating system market. But no pundit could have predicted this outcome with certainty (*United States v. Microsoft Corporation*, 253 F.3d 34 (D.C. Cir. 2001)).

Even constitutional law is to a large extent made by the Supreme Court. Consider the 14th Amendment:

> Section 1. All persons born or naturalized in the United States, and subject to the jurisdiction thereof, are citizens of the United States and of the State wherein they reside. No State shall make or enforce any law which shall abridge the privileges or immunities of citizens of the United States; *nor shall any State deprive any person of life, liberty, or property, without due process of law*; nor deny to any person within its jurisdiction the equal protection of the laws. [Emphasis added]

In *Roe v. Wade*, 410 U.S. 113 (1973), the Supreme Court recognized the right to an abortion as a fundamental right included within the guarantee of personal privacy, which is in turn protected under the due process provision of the 14th Amendment. In the Supreme Court's view, the right to have an abortion could only be limited to the extent there is a "compelling state interest". Most experts recognize that the court's "interpretation" of the Constitution goes way beyond the original meaning of the text. Therefore, constitutional law is also largely judge-made law.

At the other side, there is federal statute law with detailed provisions that reduce the role of judges. Examples include the Federal Arbitration Act, the Bankruptcy Code, and the Civil Rights Act (including the famous Title VII forbidding discrimination). There is also detailed regulation concerning finance and securities. The Uniform Commercial Code (UCC), although technically state law (more on that later), contains many detailed provisions as well.

At first glance, the important role American courts play stands in strong contrast with the role of courts in civil law countries. The difference may be less extreme than it looks though because civil law judges make a lot of law under the form of "interpretations". Take tort law for example. The Napoleonic Civil Code of 1804 devoted less than a page to tort law (Articles 1382–1386). Yet French tort law could easily fill up a treatise of 5,000 pages. Who made the other 4,999 pages? The higher French courts, and especially the highest court, the Court de Cassation. But they never admitted that they made tort rules—all the time they pretended to just "interpret" the original Napoleonic Code. French courts did not make law openly—they frame it as mere "interpretations" of vague terms like the word "fault" in Article 1382 of the Napoleonic Code: "Any human act which causes damage to another obliges the person through whose *fault* it occurred to make reparation." [Italics added]

3. American litigation relies on juries

Many civil law countries, like the Netherlands, never use juries. Other civil law countries, like France, Belgium, Austria, Italy, Greece, Russia, Argentina or Japan, use juries but only for the most serious crimes.

This stands in contrast to the U.S., where plaintiffs and defendants have a right to demand a jury trial in both criminal and civil cases. The right to demand a jury trial has been written into the United States Constitution as well as in the Constitution of most states. The U.S. Constitution, Seventh Amendment states:

> In suits at *common law*, where the value in controversy shall exceed twenty dollars, the right of trial by jury shall be preserved, and no fact tried by a jury, shall be otherwise re-examined in any Court of the United States, than according to the rules of the common law. [Emphasis added]

According to the New York Constitution art. I, § 2: "Trial by jury in all cases in which it has heretofore been guaranteed by constitutional provision shall remain inviolate forever; . . .".

Related: American procedure: appeal is only possible for legal error, not factual error. In civil law countries, appellate courts look at mistakes with respect to the law and the facts. The idea is to do the procedure all over again, this time not by one judge but by three judges. Because it is a brand-new trial, new factual evidence may be presented and new legal claims may be formulated.

In the U.S., appeal is only possible for an incorrect application of the law, not for factual error. The underlying idea is that the jury consists of 12 people, so that factual errors are likely small.

The importance of settlement. While litigation may ultimately lead to a jury trial, this does not happen very often. In practice, parties settle their claims. Settlement is much more common in the U.S. than in civil law countries. What explains this? One factor is that a full trial is so costly, therefore more money can be saved by settling. Another factor is that there is an extensive discovery stage, after which all parties see all the evidence, so that they can predict who has the best chance of winning. Another factor is related to contingent fees. These fees imply that the lawyer is paid only if the case is won for the client, and the payment is a percentage of the amount at stake. These fees give an incentive to the lawyer to settle as early as possible. Still another factor is the wide availability of alternative dispute resolution possibilities. A final factor may be the business-minded culture of the Americans, who reason more pragmatically.

4. American law is state law

As the name suggests, the United States of America is a union of states. The U.S. is a truly federalist country. Although the federal institutions have taken over some power of state institutions over time, it is still the case that most law is state law. According to the "enumerated powers doctrine" of Article I Section 8 of the Constitution, all issues have to be decided at the state level except for those issues that are explicitly conveyed to the federal government in the U.S. Constitution. In practice, most federal legislation is related to interstate commerce, see U.S. Constitution Article I Section 8:

> The Congress shall have Power . . . To regulate Commerce with foreign Nations, and among the several States, and with the Indian Tribes; . . . To make all Laws which shall be necessary and proper for carrying into Execution the foregoing Powers, and all other Powers vested by this Constitution in the Government of the United States, or in any Department or Officer thereof; . . .

So, there is no such thing as American contract law—each of the 50 states has its own contract law. What do professors teach then in contracts classes? They teach the rules that are most common among the 50 American states. Sometimes, they even teach conflicting rules, explaining that some states use rule A while other states use rule B.

Another implication is that a bar exam deals with the specific rules of that state. The reasoning is that it is not because you know the details of California law that you know enough New York law to practice in New York State. To make it a little easier (for JD students, not for LL M students who don't qualify to take the bar exam in many states), 33 states have now a uniform "Multistate Essay Examination".

That being said, there was such a thing as American federal contract law before 1938. Consider the famous case of *Laidlaw v. Organ*. In 1814, the price for tobacco was low in New Orleans because the English blocked the port. On 24 December 1814 the peace treaty of Ghent (a city that is now in Belgium) was signed, ending the war between England and the U.S. However, there were no telephones or telegrams at that time, so it took several months to bring the news from Ghent to New Orleans by boat. Organ knew someone on that boat and heard the news a few hours before it was publicly announced in the city. He quickly bought 111 barrels of tobacco at the low price. When Laidlaw heard the news a few hours later, he refused to deliver the tobacco.

The case was decided by the Supreme Court of the United States, and the majority opinion was written by Justice Marshall. The opinion stated that, in principle, parties don't have to disclose information in arm's length negotiations unless there is some fraud. This is now considered a pure state law case.

Until the *Erie* case in 1938, federal courts who were competent because of diversity jurisdiction (i.e., when the two parties came from different states and one of them wanted a federal court to have equal ground) created their own legal rules. In the *Erie* case, however, this was abolished by the U.S. Supreme Court on the argument that it led to forum shopping. Indeed, plaintiffs often had the choice between American law applied in a federal court, or state law applied in a state court, and they would simply choose the law that gave the better outcome for their clients.

This changed with *Erie Railroad Co. v. Tompkins*, 304 U.S. 64 (1938). The *Erie* case dealt with a railroad accident. Harry Tompkins—a citizen of Pennsylvania—was walking on a footpath alongside a railroad track in Hughestown, Pennsylvania in the middle of the night in July 1934. A train passed. An open door hit Tompkins, who fell to the ground and had his right arm crushed under the wheels of the train.

Under Pennsylvania law, Tompkins would have lost the case. Pennsylvania common law required him to prove "wanton negligence", which was hard to do. So he sued the Erie Railroad company, a New York corporation, in a federal district court in the Second Circuit under "diversity jurisdiction" (this means that the federal courts were allowed to take the case because the victim was from Pennsylvania while the injurer was from New York). The district court applied the at that time still existing federal common law (and neither New York nor Pennsylvania common law). According to federal common law, "ordinary negligence" was enough to establish liability. Tompkins won.

However, the Supreme Court of the United States reversed the decision. It argued that the system gave the plaintiff a choice between two laws. The plaintiff could forum-shop between the state court and the federal court and choose the one with the friendliest law. The Supreme Court decided it was unconstitutional for federal courts to make modifications to the substantive law of a state. As a result, when a federal judge decides cases because of diversity jurisdiction, the federal judge has to apply state law.

How about the Uniform Commercial Code, adopted in all U.S. states except Louisiana? Isn't that federal law? No, it isn't. The UCC was a model code, written by a bunch of professors, judges and law practitioners as a joint project of two non-profit organizations (the National Conference of Commissioners on Uniform State Laws and the American Law Institute). It was voluntarily adopted by the state lawmakers, sometimes with minor cosmetic changes.

What is the difference between the way the UCC was implemented and directives of the European Union? The latter are orders at the European level for member states to adapt their legal system to obtain a certain effect. Typically, the implemented versions differ between countries. The Uniform Commercial Code was not an order but a kind invitation. Also, the implementation was usually literal.

5. How to read an opinion of an American court

When a court decides, it summarizes its reasoning in the form of a text that is called an *opinion*. Reading an opinion in the U.S. is usually easier than in a civil law country for several reasons. First, many American judges make a deliberate effort to write in plain English. The plain English movement is much stronger than in other countries because the U.S. is a country that at every moment in time had a significant number of non-native immigrants in its population. (This is also related to the American culture of speaking loud and clear.) Secondly, American courts are officially allowed to make precedents, and since precedents are binding for lower courts, higher courts make sure the opinion clearly conveys the ruling. Thirdly, the fact that precedents can be made in an open way allows court to simply say what it is thinking.

Here are some other concepts you need to know before you can understand an opinion. I present them in alphabetic order.

Affidavit. This is a written and signed declaration. If it can be proven that the declaration was false, it is considered perjury and criminal sanctions may follow.

Case caption and case citation. This is the introductory part in a court paper. The case caption consists of the family name of the parties (the name is United States when the government is prosecuting someone or just a party in the case). It contains the names of the parties, the name of the court, the docket or file number, and the title of the document. For instance, in the citation *Roe v. Wade*, 410 U.S. 113 (1973), this means the case was heard by the Supreme Court of the United States; the first name is the plaintiff, the second name is the defendant; the case was published in the United States reporter volume 410 starting at page 113 and the year was 1973. In *United States v. Carroll Towing Co*, 159 F.2d 169 (2d

Cir. 1947), the case citation tells us that the case was published in volume 159 of the Federal Reporter (Second) starting at page 169, and that it was decided by the Second Circuit in 1947.

When the defendant loses the case in the first instance and goes to an appellate court, that party becomes the "appellant" and the other party becomes the "appellee". Usually, the order of the names becomes reversed, with the first name referring to the appellant, who was the defendant (and second name) at first instance.

Concurring opinion. Here one or more judges agree with the outcome, but not with the legal reasoning of the majority opinion.

De novo review. Here, a court acts as if it is the first to judge the case. In other words, the court does not give any weight to the reasoning of another court. Review is always *de novo* when appellate courts review questions of law of lower courts. Sometimes the higher court orders a trial *de novo* at the lower level in which all issues are reviewed as if it is for the first time.

Declaratory decision. A declaratory decision is the legal determination of a court that resolves legal uncertainty for the litigants and ends their controversial legal relationship. To put it another way, it is a decision clarifying the legal rights. A declaratory decision may come after a cease and desist letter. It is popular in common law countries but does not exist in civil law countries.

Demurrer. Here, the defendant does not want to dispute the factual claims of the plaintiff because the defendant is confident the plaintiff will lose on legal grounds. By doing so, the facts in the case officially become those asserted by the other party.

Dicta. This is a remark by a judge about a different issue from the one which is considered in a case. It comes from Latin, *obiter dicta*, which literally means "by the way said". It is a remark in the style of, "By the way, if you would ever bring a case to me about issue X, then rule A is what I would apply." Dicta is not binding, although it contains some direction on future litigation. You may compare this to dissenting opinions which obviously do not bind but may serve as an invitation to bring a case with a certain fact pattern to the court.

Dissenting opinion. Here, one or more judges *disagree* with the outcome—and therefore usually also with the legal reasoning of the majority opinion. Does publishing dissenting opinions undermine legal certainty? It is probably the opposite. Dissenting opinions give insight into the true reasoning of judges, and therefore make it easier to predict new precedents.

Distinguishing cases. If two cases are similar but the outcome is different, you have to argue why the cases are different enough to warrant a different outcome. Take *Lucy v. Zehmer* in which Zehmer was joking about selling his farm. Zehmer lost the case. Compare this to *Leonard v. Pepsico*, in which Pepsico was joking about giving a military airplane to anyone who collected 7,000,000 Pepsi points. Zehmer lost but Pepsico won. Is this consistent or can we distinguish the two cases? The cases can be distinguished: a reasonable person would have believed Zehmer was serious and Pepsico was joking.

Diversity jurisdiction. In principle, state law must be decided by state courts. Local parties, however, may have a home court advantage. To prevent that, the party from a different state may file the case to a federal court. This court is then competent because of *diversity jurisdiction*.

Federal-question jurisdiction. Here, the federal court is competent to take on the case because the claim is related to the application of federal law. For instance, a claim about the validity of an arbitration clause may be filed with a federal court because the issue is related to the application of the Federal Arbitration Act.

Holding. The holding is the sentence(s) in which the rule is formulated. Consider *United States v. Carroll Towing Co.* (1947), in which Judge Learned Hand formulated the famous Learned Hand Formula, which defines negligence in tort law as the failure to take precautions when the precaution costs are smaller than the expected accident costs. The holding can be found in the following passage from *United States v. Carroll Towing Co.*, 159 F.2d 169 (2d Cir. 1947):

> the owner's duty . . . to provide against resulting injuries is a function of three variables: (1) the probability that she will break away; (2) the gravity of the resulting injury, if she does; (3) the burden of adequate precautions. Possibly it serves to bring this notion into relief to state it in algebraic terms: if the

probability be called P; the injury, L; and the burden, B; liability depends upon whether B is less than L multiplied by P, i.e., whether B < PL.

Legal pseudonyms. Some international students feel that the explicit use of the original names violates the privacy of the parties. Some American courts allow the name to be changed. Typically, names like Roe or Doe are taken. For instance, in the case *Roe v. Wade*, the woman seeking a right to an abortion chose the legal pseudonym "Jane Roe". She later identified herself as Norma McCorvey when she wrote a book about her own story, see Norma McCorvey and Andy Meisler, *I Am Roe* (New York, Harper Collins, 1994).

Majority opinion. This is the opinion of the majority of the judges. One of the unique characteristics of common law courts is indeed that outsiders get a clear view of the political process within a court. Civil law courts, in contrast, always write opinions as if there was unanimity.

Motion for summary judgment. This is a motion asking that the court rules for one party against another without a full trial. According to Rule 56 of the Federal Rules of Civil Procedure, any party has right to move for summary judgment before 30 days after the close of discovery. The court will grant summary judgment motions once the moving party shows that (1) there is no genuine factual dispute, and (2) the moving party is entitled to judgment as a matter of law. Here, one of the parties argues that presenting the case to a jury is a waste of time as the facts are clear enough. The court can move on and decide the case regarding the legal issues.

Motion to dismiss. Here, the defendant argues that a jury trial should not be started because even if the jury would consider the plaintiff's factual assertions proven, the plaintiff would lose on legal grounds. Basically, the defendant says, "Judge, let's not waste our time, please decide now that the plaintiff can't win on legal grounds." Dismissal may be *with prejudice*, which means that refiling is not allowed, or *without prejudice*, in which case the plaintiff may refile the claim on better legal grounds.

Reverse and decide. What can a higher court decide, outside of simply affirming the decision of the lower court? If the higher court overturns a lower court's decision, it may decide the case if no new facts need to be proven. This differs from French law, for instance, where the highest court has to send back the case to a lower court even if all the facts are known. The idea is that the highest French court is a cassation court, so that it can only affirm or break a decision. That being said, American law looks more efficient (and faster) in such cases. Why give the lower court unnecessary work?

Reverse and remand. If new facts need to be found, the higher court reverses the decision and sends it back to the same trial court. The underlying idea is that higher courts have less time than lower courts and are not specialized in fact gathering either.

6. Langdell and the Socratic method at American law schools

The typical teaching method at American law schools is usually described as the Socratic method. It was conceived by Christopher Langdell, the dean of the Harvard Law School from 1870–95. To better understand Langdell's teaching method, we need to understand his underlying reasoning.

In 1870, American universities were considered inferior to European universities. There was especially admiration for German universities, which were believed to be more scientific. Langdell liked the German ideal of law as a science in itself, forming one logical unity. He also liked the rigorously scientific teaching method.

However, he felt that the German deductive method was too far away from the English inductive tradition. In the deductive method, professors first explain abstract concepts (like "legal act" or "obligation") and then derive intermediate concepts, and eventually derive detailed rules, all through deduction. Common law judges, in Langdell's view, did not work deductively but inductively, starting with concrete cases and reasoning up to the more general underlying principles that were extrapolated from cases.

The compromise Langdell came up with was to produce a book with selected cases. Students would memorize those cases and try to find the principles behind them. The idea was that if students had studied enough carefully selected cases, they would have the knowledge to later solve all legal problems. The law practitioner would just ask what the closest case was and apply the underlying principle on the current fact pattern.

Langdell's own *Selection of Cases on the Law of Contracts* (1871) was the first book using the new case method. After 1890 other law schools started to copy Langdell's method. Soon a similar evolution took place in medical schools, where Johns Hopkins University (founded in 1876) became the first research university, the first to teach through seminars (instead of through only lectures) and the first to make medical studies rigorously scientific. Washington University Medical School was one of the first to copy this model.

Although the method is called the Socratic method, it differs from Socrates' teaching method. At law schools, the professor only asks questions. These questions push the students to think until they find the correct legal principles underneath the cases. Is this Socratic? Well, Socrates asked questions but also launched hypotheses. The method could more accurately be described as the Freudian method, where a psychiatrist only wants to hold a mirror for the patient by asking the right questions.

7. How to prepare for classes and exams at American law schools

How to prepare for class. Law school is all about reading fast, thinking fast, and writing fast. So when you are preparing for class, your criterion for success is not only whether you can identify the main facts and arguments but also how fast you read the case. In practice, this means going quickly over all parts and then reading a few passages more slowly.

Usually, there are two types of students who initially spend too much time to prepare for classes in law school. The first are the international students who are used to studying dense textbooks, in which every word is important. The second are the American science students, who are trained to take every word, even every symbol, extremely seriously. Keep in mind that American casebooks are different. Students are expected to skim loads of texts. The art of fast reading is the art of discovering quickly what the most important passages are.

How much information should you memorize for class? You should always have an *elevator version* of the facts. An elevator version is a summary in about 15 seconds—enough to answer a question about the case while the elevator goes from floor 1 to floor 4. You should also have an elevator version of the holding (i.e., of the judge-made law used to decide the case).

Some professors want you to analyse a case using the IRAC method. IRAC is an acronym that stands for Issue, Rule, Application, and Conclusion. It is generally suggested that law students' legal analysis should begin with an indication of the issue. For instance, if the rule is "simple negligence", the issue may be "what type of negligence needs to be proven?" Then, students should know the law (the R from "Rule") and the facts (the

A from "Application") and then apply the law to the facts. Finally, based on comprehensive analysis, students should reach their conclusion (the C from "Conclusion").

When you memorize the facts, delete all details that do not matter. The shorter your own summary is, the longer you will remember it. Don't use "plaintiff" or "defendant" in your summary, unless the course is about procedure. Use "baker" and "consumer" instead, or other descriptions of the reality that are easier to visualize and therefore easier to remember.

How to prepare for the exams. Most exams consist of *fact patterns*, which is just a fancy term for stories that deal with what happened to a fictitious personage (who is your imaginary client). Students must spot all legally relevant issues and give a prediction of the most likely court decision. Bar exams partly consist of such fact patterns as well.

There may be a difference between preparing for class and preparing for the exam. For class, you may want to memorize detailed facts of the cases. For the exam, all you need is to memorize the elevator version of the cases discussed in class, plus the definition of concepts. In addition, you must memorize the "tests" of the doctrines. For instance, when you discuss unconscionability, you must know that you have to find both procedural and substantive unconscionability in most jurisdictions.

However, the situation is different for an open book exam. Also, compared to civil law countries, students don't need to memorize a great deal for class or exams. American law schools rely on analysis far more than on memorization.

Fact pattern exams are largely speed tests. You must remember to read fast, think fast and write fast. In essence, these exams mimic the situation of law firms. After all, there is usually a limit to billable hours—so a good lawyer is someone who can get a lot of work done in a short amount of time.

How should you prepare for such tests? By writing short pieces every single day, trying to improve your ability to write in plain English and your ability to type fast.

Take-home test and moveable-date test. International students are often surprised to hear that some exams give the students 24 hours for completion and the right to work anywhere. Doesn't this lead to students helping each other? International students are surprised that some shorter exams can be taken at any time during the exam period and that all students receive the same questions. Doesn't this lead to students passing on the exam questions to their friends who take the exam later?

Keep in mind that American law schools have a strict honors code—so you really must do the exam on your own. If an honors code violation is discovered, it may be difficult to even get accepted at the bar of your choice. American culture puts much emphasis on honesty.

Writing a paper at an American law school. According to the accreditation rules of the American Bar Association, 35-page-long papers (double-spaced, Times New Roman, 12 pt.) are typically required for three credits. This is the number of pages if the seminar consists only of writing a paper. If there are also classes, fewer pages are required. Still, that is a lot of pages. Also here, success depends on the ability to read fast, think fast and write fast.

Plagiarism. Plagiarism rules are much stricter in the U.S. than in other countries. This is related to universalist ethics and to the strong private property culture—so that copying is quickly considered stealing.

For instance, if you take over the complete structure of another paper, that may constitute plagiarism. If you literally take over a single sentence without quotation marks, that can be considered plagiarism as well. Writing the source in a footnote is not enough—this stands in stark contrast to the rules in many other countries. The reason is that the footnote may mean that the underlying ideas are supported by the referenced publication, this way concealing that the exact structure or wording was also taken over. In short, either you quote or you paraphrase.

Make sure you don't unintentionally plagiarize. When you make notes, always make sure you put them in quotation marks when you literally copy text and always make clear what is not your own text.

Bar exams test old legal knowledge. In the U.S., as in most other countries, finishing law school is not enough to become an attorney—candidates must also pass the bar exam. Most American students take a bar preparation course, like Kaplan or Barbri. This preparation course deals with the same subjects as those offered at law school (contracts, property, sale of goods, etc.) but in a different way. Why don't law professors teach students to be fully prepared for the bar exam? Because national law schools (that recruit mostly beyond their own state) in principle will tell you that they don't directly prepare for the bar exam.

To understand why, consider three of the most important concepts of contract law, all produced by 20th century scholars: (1) the distinction between the expectation measure and the reliance measure (Fuller and Perdue, 1936); (2) the least-cost information gatherer principle of Kronman (1978); and (3) the superior-risk bearer concept of Posner and Rosenfield (1977). Which of these three concepts do you have to know at the bar exam?

The answer is: only the first. Follow-up question: why? Because the other two are too recent. Bar exams test only old legal knowledge.

This may sound like a joke, but it isn't. Bar exams do test current law, but there are many ways to describe current law. In bar exams they want you to describe current law using the older concepts, not the more recent ones. For contract law, more recent means developed after 1962–79, which is the time span in which the Restatement was written. So in practice, literature up to somewhere in the mid-1970s could be taken into account. As a result, you have to know the distinction between the expectation measure and the reliance measure, which was introduced by Fuller and Purdue in a law review article in the 1930s, and which found its way into the Restatement. But you do not have to know the least-costs information gatherer principle of Kronman and the superior-risk bearer concept of Posner and Rosenfield, which were all introduced in the late 1970s, after most of the Restatement (Second) was written. So, while the more recent decisions of higher state or federal courts do find their way to the summaries of contract law in your state, these summaries use the conceptual framework of the Restatement (Second).

The fact that you do not have to know any new contract law insight published during the last four and a half decades has a couple of implications. The first is that when you prepare for the bar exam, you can forget everything your law and economics minded professor told you. Law and economics started to grow in the 1970s. That is too late for the current bar exams.

The second is that the students' success at bar exams is somewhat of a mixed indicator for the quality of the law school. This success tells you how well students are familiar with the insights from before 1970 but it does not tell you how much they picked up of the more recent literature. Strictly speaking a law school that only wants to prepare its students for the bar exam could save big on library books—there is no need to buy anything that was published after the most recent Restatement.

PART II

Understanding American legal culture

8. The theory of Glaeser and Shleifer

Why do common law countries rely heavily on juries, while civil law countries rely on professional judges? Glaeser and Shleifer (2002) have an interesting theory on why England and France developed different systems from the 12th century onwards.

The starting point is that kings are naturally not interested in solving legal disputes. Kings would rather have the people solve their own disputes, using a jury of peers. A local jury system, however, can only function when jury members are not put under pressure through threats or bribes. In France, that was a problem in late medieval times. Feudal local lords were so powerful that they feared each other more than they feared the king. In those circumstances, a jury system could not work.

When a jury can't work because of local pressure, the only solution is to leave the adjudication to someone who is even more powerful than the local lord—the king. The king is the only person strong enough to withstand local pressure. But the king himself has no time to travel around adjudicating all disputes in the entire country; he has to send employees to work as local judges. Unfortunately, that creates another problem—the local judge could be put under local pressure as well.

Therefore, the king distrusted his own judges and needed to set up a system to monitor them. One way was to set up appellate courts, typically in a different city, away from the original location. Those courts needed to check not only whether the local judge correctly applied the law (because he may deliberately have misapplied the law to let a powerful party win) but also whether he correctly found the facts (because he may have misreported the facts to let that powerful party win). To the extent that there were local customs, the king wanted to codify them to prevent the local judge from misrepresenting the local customs in order to let that powerful party win. Another way to supervise local judges was to make them put as much as possible in writing.

In England, the situation was different. After Willem the Conqueror won the Battle of Hastings in 1066, he wiped out the existing feudal power structure and gave smaller lots of land to the new class of nobility.

Of course, some form of quality control was necessary here because jury members may not know the law. The appeals process, however, could be limited to questions of law; for factual questions, the appellate court could rely on the jury. This is what happened in England.

Glaeser and Shleifer's theory is interesting, not only because it models French law as a top-down management system, but also because it explains many typical features of French law: hardly any juries, more written evidence, emphasis on codification with bright line rules, inquisitorial system (most evidence collected prior to the trial by a judge-inquisitor), appeals review both law and evidence. However, its explanation is incomplete because it only explains why the system became like this and not why the system remained like this long after the initial cause disappeared.

9. Universalism versus particularism

Universalism and particularism refer to opposite cultural dimensions. In universalism, the highest ethical norm is truthfulness and fairness towards *all* people, irrespective of whether they are your friends or not. In particularism, in contrast, the highest ethical norm is to help your own friends and relatives.

Suppose your friend gives you a ride, but he drives recklessly fast and accidentally hits a pedestrian. A police officer asks you what happened. Would you tell the truth and get your friend in trouble? Or would you lie to protect your friend? Universalists do the former, while particularists do the latter. As it turns out, Switzerland, the U.S., England, Scandinavia and Germany have an outspokenly universalist culture. In contrast, Russia, South Korea, Venezuela and China have a largely particularistic culture. France is somewhere in the middle.

Which one is better? Each has advantages and disadvantages. Russians feel that Americans and Scandinavians can't be trusted because the latter would betray even their best friends. Americans and Scandinavians feel that Russians can't be trusted because Russians want to do favors for their friends rather than apply the rules.

Where do those cultural differences come from? Universalism is strongly correlated with a long democratic tradition. Particularism is strongly correlated with centuries of exploitative dictatorship. Universalists take the law seriously because the law is seen as fair. Particularists have experienced that the law is often unfair, and therefore focus on helping each other, even against the legal system.

Those cultural differences may explain why the French legal system does not trust individual citizens or local judges: citizens or local officers may help their friends rather than do what is in the general interest of society. Universalism may also explain why common law countries can use a bottom-up approach: those at the bottom can be trusted because they would rather do what is fair than what is in the interest of their friends.

What are the general consequences for the law? First, countries with a strong universalist culture (like the U.S.) have a higher enforcement factor. In other words, there is a smaller difference between the law-on-the-books and the law-in-action because moral norms push toward enforcement.

Secondly, universalists like written contracts. Moreover, they like lengthy contracts. For them, a long contract is a sign of someone who will stick to what has been agreed to. For particularists, a lengthy contract is a sign of distrust. Would you let your best friend sign a contract? If a friend needs that, they are not a real friend, or so goes the reasoning. When universalists visit a doctor, they don't philosophically object against having to sign consents to treat or privacy notices. Particularists get uneasy because of all that paperwork.

Thirdly, and more broadly, universalists are bothered by lying even to strangers. They love disclosure requirements. Particularists don't love lying but they are not shocked by it. They see it as a part of life.

Also, when there is a conflict in a particularist culture, the restoration of the friendship is more important than the application of the correct legal rule.

This is colorfully illustrated by the following anecdote (Daniel S. Lev, "Judicial Institutions and Legal Culture in Indonesia", in Claire Holt (ed), *Culture and Politics in Indonesia* (1972, pp. 283–87). An American checked into a hotel in Indonesia. He went to the bathroom of his room. There he pulled the flush but he got the whole toilet on himself. He went to the owner of the hotel to complain and ask for compensation, but the owner said that the guest had to pay for destroying the restroom. The American went to court. There, after the parties had explained the facts, the judge took the American to one side in his private chamber. The judge said that the American was right but that he refused to decide the case. Instead the American had to offer to pay half of the restroom to the owner. This anecdote illustrates that in a particularist country like Indonesia, restoring the relationship is culturally more important than the exact rule being applied.

10. Bottom-up versus top-down legal systems

Americans believe that decentralized, local decision making is better than top-down decision making. They distrust the federal government in Washington, D.C. They distrust their own state government more than their own city government. They distrust the city more than their neighbors or themselves.

This is different in France. French people have more trust in whatever is higher in the hierarchy. They have more trust in their president than in their neighbors. They have more trust in the government than in the courts, and more trust in the higher courts than in the lower courts. They have more trust in Paris than Americans have in Washington, D.C.

If there is a problem in the country, the French entrust their own president and national government to come up with a solution.

This top-down approach leads to a concentration of power. There is no federalism in France—political power is concentrated at the national level, and provinces (*departements*) and cities have very limited autonomy. The president chooses the prime minister and the Parliament usually approves the proposals of the government.

This stands in sharp contrast with the U.S. First, the U.S. is a purely federalist country, where federal power is the exception and state power the rule. Most law is made at a state level. In France, by contrast, the provinces and cities have little power. Nearly all power is concentrated at the central level.

Secondly, American court proceedings are adversarial. This means that the parties take the lead in procedure. So, the parties lead, not the official judge. In France (and even more clearly so in Germany), the judge leads the trial.

Thirdly, class actions are common in the U.S. but nearly non-existent in civil law countries. Class actions mean that a lawyer of a few individuals leads law enforcement. A consumer (or her lawyer) plays the role of "private attorney-general". Such collective enforcement is seen as a job for the public prosecutor in civil law countries.

Fourthly, whistleblowers are often used and encouraged by bounties in the U.S. So, an individual does a part of the prosecutor's work, not the prosecutor. In the old days of the Wild West, boards with "Wanted, dead or alive" granted high monetary awards to individuals who helped arrest a criminal.

Fifthly, punitive damages (more on that later) give incentives to individuals to go after wrongdoers. Punitive damages can be seen as soft criminal law. A private party receives an amount of money that would in another legal system be a fine paid to the government.

Sixthly, there are more checks and balances in the U.S. than in France.

Finally, one reason why gun rights are forcefully defended by many Americans is the notion that individuals sometimes have to rely on themselves for their safety, rather than on government-paid police officers.

11. Procedural formalism

One ambitious empirical study in cooperation with Lex Mundi member law firms in 109 countries described the exact procedures litigants have to follow to evict a tenant for nonpayment of rent and to collect a bounced check. The study found that formalism is systematically greater in civil than in common law countries, and is associated with higher expected duration of judicial proceedings, less consistency, less honesty, less fairness in judicial decisions and more corruption.

To see how lack of trust of individuals leads to formalism, suppose you own a consultancy firm with many employees. How should employees proceed when they need to order a book for a project? If you fully trust them—that is, if you know that they will only order books they absolutely need for the project and never books they only want for their personal entertainment or development—then you will use an informal system. You will tell your employees something like: "If you want to order a book, please don't bother me. I have more important tasks to focus on. Just order it, and I will reimburse the costs without even checking." If, in contrast, you do not trust them, you will install a formalistic system, and require them to fill out a form which needs to be rubber-stamped personally by you beforehand. You will also announce that under no circumstances will expenses be reimbursed when this procedure is not followed.

French law is very formalistic. Why? Because the culture is largely particularistic—there is a real friend-helps-friend danger. As a result, the top does not trust judges, individual citizens, lower civil servants and even higher courts.

To further entertain my readers, I present an illustration of the formalistic nature of the French legal tradition—a story of what really happened in an adoption procedure at a Belgian court a couple of years ago. All legal systems have some form of monitoring on adoption because there is the (at least theoretical) danger that an adopted child was sold, or stolen, or adopted to be used as a cheap workforce, or adopted by parents who are unable to provide a loving and nurturing environment. The Belgian adoption act describes in an extremely detailed way the type of evidence the judges need to collect, the form in which the evidence needs to be collected, the stage of the procedure at which it needs to be collected and even what the judges need to mention in their decisions.

One day, an agent of an adoption organization entered the court room and handed over a single, 12-page report. "This is not enough, you need to give us four reports", said the judge. "But the four reports are integrated into that single report", answered the adoption agent. "You will see that there are four sections of three pages each, and section 1 contains the information of report 1, section 2 corresponds to report 2, etc." "Still", said the judge, "this is not in accordance with the law, which mentions the documents separately; therefore, I will have to postpone the case".

The word "postpone" strikes fear in everybody's hearts, because Belgian law is famous for its long judicial delays (and this is no coincidence, but a typical feature of most countries within the French family). The adoption agent requested a 30-minute break, ran to his car, opened his laptop, split the Word file into four separate files, ran to a printer shop and arrived at the court just in time, out of breath. "Now you have followed the law", said the judge, and five minutes later the adoption was approved.

Now, this is what I call formalism! Why does the legislator describe in detail what judges have to do, including the type of evidence they need to ask for and the form in which it has to be delivered? Because the legislator does not trust judges! If there were full trust, the legislator would let the judges decide what type of evidence is helpful in each individual situation!

To be fair, it is not definite that the members of Parliament who voted in the adoption act would have wanted the adoption agent to split the file into four files in this case. But this is one of the problems of formalism: there is usually no communication line between those who make the rules and those who apply them. When in doubt, Belgian judges tend to prefer the stricter interpretation, because it is better for their career to be known as overly strict than as overly lax.

12. German law

In Germany, determining the law is seen as a "scientific" activity. That sounds great. Ask a German professor a legal question and she will give you the "scientifically correct" answer. A German law professor is a "legal scientist". She will not tell you whether the law is good or bad—that is not her role, but rather the role of the political or philosophical department. And because German law is so "scientific", it should come as no surprise that its Civil Code (BGB) is technical and hard to read.

Is there anything wrong with this viewpoint? Well, if the law were complete, then determining the "legal answer" could be a matter of scientifically describing the "Is". But the problem is that the law is never complete. To the contrary, law is more similar to Emmental cheese than it is to Gouda—it is always full of gaps. Filling those gaps can never be a scientific activity, because scientists can only describe the existing reality (the "Is"), not the ideal reality (the "Ought"). If there is no law on a certain issue, the question is not what the law is, but what the law should be. This is a "political" activity, if politics is defined in a broad way (determining policy) and not in a narrow way (the set of policy questions that most members of Parliament find interesting).

More generally, there is a strong universalist ethic in Germany. Why, then, isn't the German legal system like the American?

German law is a system where judges and law professors are scared to death of making political statements. As a result, they act as if law is a matter of pure science and logic. And because truly critical thinking about the law is lacking, legal innovation is modest in Germany as well.

Why are German lawyers so afraid of "political" positions that they basically say, "don't shoot me, I am only a scientist"? To explain this, we have to go back in history. Before 1870, Germany was not a single, united country (like France), but a set of small countries, sometimes not much larger than a city. At a certain point, Germany consisted of 300 separate countries.

Applying the theory of Glaeser and Shleifer, it is obvious that a jury-based common law system could not work here, because of the presence of an extremely powerful local lord. The French solution was to let the king decide, but in Germany there was no strong "king" (formally there was a *Kaiser*, but his power was too weak).

How do you build up a legal system under those circumstances? By making the law as general, abstract and neutral-looking as possible. Not surprisingly, Roman law had a greater impact in Germany than in any other legal system (outside Italy). Roman law allowed lawyers to be neutral scientists. They could limit their advice to giving the correct answer under Roman law. Basically, lawyers could say to the powerful local lord that they really regretted that his friends lost the case, but that they were not allowed to make any statements on what is fair, only on what is "scientifically correct" according to Roman law. They were only scientists, bringing the message, and you don't shoot at scientists just like you don't shoot at messengers.

To illustrate how problematic the local pressure on judges and lawyers was, consider a typical feature of old German law—*Aktenversendung*. Under this practice (which became common in the late 17th century), a German court asked an external legal expert to write a draft decision (literally by "sending the files of the case"). The draft decision was in theory just an advice but in practice binding. Why would the court not rely on its own legal expertise? Because the court was too afraid to take a position if one of the parties was closely related to the local lord. In the beginning, the files were sent to a single professor of a law school of another jurisdiction. But after a while, professors only wanted to give advice if it formally came from the entire faculty. And in some cases, entire faculties only wanted to give advice if the identity of the law school was hidden to the parties of the case!

German law students learn to be proud of German law because it is scientific, apolitical, neutral and based on general principles of logic. Some state courts in the U.S. (for instance, the Missouri courts) have the same German culture, priding themselves on being politically neutral, just applying the law, and being the opposite of activist judges.

13. Religion, ethics, and law

What is the relationship between religion, ethics, and law? That varies among different regions of the world.

In the Islamic world, religion equals ethics and ethics equals the law. The Koran answers not only religious questions like how to pray and whether there is life after this life, but also questions on what to do, without specifying whether it is a mere moral command or a legal command. In principle, it is both. So, religion equals ethics equals law.

At the other end of the spectrum stands the East Asian culture. Here, religion differs from ethics, and ethics in turn differs from law. A typical East Asian religion tells you something about life after death, but offers less practical guidance on what to do in this life than, for instance, Christianity or Islam. Ethicists like Confucius tell us what to do in daily life but little about what happens after death. So, ethics and religion are decoupled. Law, in turn, is whatever the emperor decides. There is no strict connection between ethics and the law. Religion is not ethics and is not law.

In the middle stands the Western Christian tradition. Religion and ethics are closely related (Jesus Christ tells us what to do in daily situations), but law differs from religion and ethics. The idea is that there is a difference between what you have to do according your conscience versus what you have to do according to the law.

The Western, Christian view was partly the outcome of the religious wars and the Peace Treaty of Westphalia in 1648. That treaty stated that religion was an internal affair for each state. Each king decided for his own state what religion was permitted and thus indirectly on what ethics to follow in his kingdom.

Still, there is a strong idea that some acts that are immoral may still be legal. This is especially strong in libertarian philosophy where the law determines who decides what to do with a certain object (for instance, who owns a dog), but the decision itself (for instance, to torture the dog) is a moral matter in which the law does not intervene.

In practice, most differences are more nuanced. For instance, Chinese civil servants who wanted to make a career had to study Confucian ethics. As a result, Chinese law was strongly influenced by ethics. Also, French rhetoric sometimes emphasizes the importance of ethics for the law.

That being said, there is a strong religious influence in civil life and the law in the U.S. This explains why you may find centers on law and religion and seminars on law and religion at American law schools.

14. Legal realism versus scholastic thinking

What is scholastics? Reasoning not in an open way. In medieval times, it was common for philosophers to conceal their own thinking behind the thinking of philosophers from the classical period. One reason was that authors of the classical period were considered smarter, or that every truth could be discovered from classic writers, if only the right passage could be found. Another reason was that medieval thinkers feared criticism. Attributing an argument to a great individual from the past reduced criticism.

The tendency not to take full responsibility for one's own thinking was even visible in St. Thomas Aquinas, a leading philosopher of the 13th century. Aquinas wanted to make the point that private property is a good thing and slavery is a bad thing. His next task was to find a quotation that would support this. For private property he cited Aristotle as the main authority (Aristotle wrote that when many servants share a good, there tends to be nobody who takes full care of it). Next, Aquinas had to find an authority who said that slavery is bad. As it turned out, Aristotle was in favor of slavery—even on racist grounds. Aristotle believed that human beings of other city states were not able to think for themselves, so that the Greeks did them a favor by thinking for them. That is not what the Italian Aquinas wanted to hear. So, when he explained that slavery is bad, he did not refer to Aristotle but to other sources.

What is typical for this way of thinking is that the quotation works as camouflage. First, the author makes a conclusion, and then he wonders, "Who could have said this?" and goes through all his books until he finds a quotation that supports it.

What is the relationship with civil law thinking? Therein lies the idea that all answers can be found in existing texts, for example legislation in this case. So when French judges decided they wanted to create precontractual liability (liability for behavior during the negotiation process when the negotiations eventually do not lead to a contract), they couldn't openly say that there were no provisions in the Napoleonic Code and that they had made it up. They had to find a "legal basis", by which they mean an Article of a piece of legislation. Therefore, they went through the Code until they found Article 1382, which states that if through your fault you cause harm then you have to pay compensation: "Any human act which causes damage to another obliges the person through whose fault it occurred to make reparation".

It was definitely not the original intent of the drafters of the Napoleonic Code to see Article 1382 as a rule that also covers precontractual liability. After all, the concept itself wasn't even known in 1804—it was invented in the late 19th century by the German legal scholar von Jhering.

This stands in sharp contrast with American opinions. Take, for instance, Judge Easterbrook's opinion in *Hill v. Gateway* (2000):

> A customer picks up the phone, orders a computer, and gives a credit card number. Presently a box arrives, containing the computer and a list of terms, said to govern unless the customer returns the computer within 30 days. Are these terms effective as the parties' contract, or is the contract term-free because the order-taker did not read any terms over the phone and elicit the customer's assent?

> . . . Payment preceding the revelation of full terms is common for air transportation, insurance, and many other endeavors. . . . If the staff at the other end of the phone for direct-sales operations such as Gateway's had to read the four-page statement of terms before taking the buyer's credit card number, the droning voice would anesthetize rather than enlighten many potential buyers. Others would hang up in a rage over the waste of their time. . . . For what little it is worth, we add that the box from Gateway was crammed with software. The computer came with an operating system, without which it was useful only as a boat anchor.

This is the style of the self-confident, creative, activist judge with no desire to camouflage his view behind a curtain of citations.

Why do civil law judges camouflage their own rulemaking? Civil law courts make law, nearly as much as American courts. Yet, they act as if they only apply legislation. Why do they do that?

Unlike common law judges, French judges cannot openly make new legal rules. The official reason is the doctrine of the separation of powers, which holds that lawmaking is a task for the legislative branch and not for the judicial branch. This explanation is not so convincing because in practice the executive branch (the president, the government) does most of the lawmaking work and this practice is generally accepted. Why can the executive branch violate the principle of the separation of powers but not the judicial branch? Because the French legal system is a top-down organization. When more power becomes concentrated at the top of such a system, that is considered to be fine, but when power moves down (to judges, who are lower in the "pecking order"), that is considered a violation. A related explanation is that judges are distrusted, but the central government is not.

A lot has to do with the anti-judge mood since the French Revolution. Judges were employees of the king, so that political revolutions against the king were also against judges. In addition, during the Ancien Regime (just before the French Revolution) French judges even refused to announce the few changes the king was willing to make. Judges did this because the changes reduced the privileges of the aristocracy, to which the judges belonged. After more than two centuries, the fear regarding "class justice", that is, court decision making that helps the leading class, is still strong.

The most typical feature of French courts is their lack of open argumentation. There is a huge gap between the official arguments given by a court (which usually take the form of "just read the Civil Code!") and the real arguments for why they preferred a certain rule (for instance, that the chosen rule is easier to administer, less prone to abuse, or more predictable). The real policy arguments are never revealed. They are officially irrelevant in the French legal system because it is not the job of judges to even consider those arguments—that is the job of politicians.

Note that this attitude is typical for top-down systems more generally. The top gives all the instructions, but the bottom wants some power, too. So, the bottom makes many decisions but reports that it just followed the instructions from the top.

Why do French professors join the French judges? Professors teach skills that make students successful professionals. Straightforward policy arguments are taboo in French courts, so there is no point in training students in making policy arguments. Instead, "interpretations" of words in legislative texts can help win a case, and therefore French professors teach students this skill.

German courts are a little more open in their argumentation, however they like to hide their policy arguments behind a scientific language. As explained, German judges developed that attitude to avoid criticism—even to guarantee their own physical safety. Sometimes, however, they openly admit that there is no law so that they have to make a precedent. Consider, for instance, the following German case. The case deals with stock lease, that is, the long-term rental of cattle. The contract had not stipulated that at the end the same number of cattle had to be given back but that cattle of the same financial value had to be given back. Because of high inflation after World War I, the question was whether the amount had to be adapted to the inflation.[1]

German Reichsgerichthof (RG), 27 June 1922:

> The collapse of the German currency is so major that governing lease arrangements according to the provisions of § 589 (III) makes stock maintenance impossible. The gold mark which served as the basis for valuing the stock and the paper mark on the basis of which compensation is to be calculated are in no wise comparable, notwithstanding the financial parity established by the law.
>
> Neither the legal provisions nor contractual provisions enable the dispute to be resolved. The courts must be creative and deliver a judgment which accords with equity. The guiding principle must be that an equitable adjustment of the interests at stake must be made. The motives of the parties in light of the pre-war economic situation must be taken into consideration. In the present case, the extent of the stock was not in itself altered (that is to say neither increased nor diminished).
>
> Thus the lessor may not be obliged to pay sums greater than one million RM on return of the stock solely on account of the impressive rise in prices. The value of the stock increased by only 2%. It is that added value in respect of which an obligation arises for the lessor. The economic and legal principles elaborated by the RG must be observed by the courts trying the issues of fact. A decision taking into account the interests of the parties must be adopted.

Legal realism means, "let's be realistic about everything in the legal system. Let's admit that courts make legal rules, and that their decisions are based

---

[1]   English translation is from von Mehren and Gordley, *The Civil Law System*, 2nd edn (Boston, Mass, Little Brown, 1977) 1080–5.

on policy arguments". The father of legal realism, Oliver Holmes, said in *The Path of the Law* (1897): "The prophecies of what the courts will do in fact, and nothing more pretentious, are what I mean by the law." In *The Common Law* (1881) he said, "The life of the law has not been logic; it has been experience."

Holmes also said that the best way to understand the law is to look through the eyes of a bad man, who doesn't care about ethics but only about the punishment and the chance to receive it.

One form of legal realism is economic analysis of law (or "law and economics"). It means, let's be realistic and see how courts maximize welfare.

At its core, legal realism is a reaction against the black letter approach to law, against the viewpoint that law is applied to facts in a syllogistic (mechanical, formalistic) way, against the idea that law is a complete system, and against the idea that law is an autonomous system.

15. Parental legal systems

Suppose you feel that one of your kids has done something wrong. You will be the one who interrogates the kid. You will also be the one who decides on the punishment. You are the prosecutor and the judge. You apply an inquisitorial system at home. You will not accept that your child hires an attorney.

Does this lead to abuses? Probably not, because you are not a self-interested maximizer nor a sadist, but a loving parent who wants the best for her children. You have high ethical standards because it is not for you but for the betterment of the kids. As a prosecutor, you do not want to just maximize the punishment. You are more interested in the child feeling guilty, and in the child realizing what he or she did wrong. In legal terms, you want a confession (i.e., your child taking responsibility for his or her actions).

Also, you want to educate your child. You want your child to confess because you are more interested in their long-term behavior and without a feeling of guilt, behavior won't change.

Traditional Chinese law as parental law. Political opponents of Mao were often sent to a re-education camp. This was seen by some as a typical communist measure. However, Mao did only what many Chinese emperors before him had done. The Chinese system was essentially a parental adjudication system, leading to an inquisitorial system.[1] But the organization itself had an ethical mission and did not want to apply punishment for the sake of punishment.

---

[1]   Thomas B. Stephens, "Order and Discipline in China: The Shanghai Mixed Court, 1911–1927" (1994) 138 The China Quarterly 549–51.

The inquisition as a parental system. The law of the Catholic Church is also parental. The poster child of the inquisitorial method was the inquisition of non-Catholics. The inquisition was applied with a lot of ethics in the mix. Indeed, the prosecutor was a religious person on an ethical mission. Confession and re-education is central. Even dangerous criminals deserved a chance to have their souls saved.

American law is 0% parental. In the U.S., the prosecutor has an arm's length relationship with the accused. The prosecutor maximizes sentences, using all legal means. The accused is a grown-up who has to defend himself or make sure he has counsel who does a good job. It is a fight between two grown-ups. The idea is that if the two are doing an equally good job, a fair sanction will be the outcome.

16. Project-based corporate culture

I once had a student who wrote a paper on dismissal practices in the film industry in Florida. Her fiancé, a specialist in drawing thumbs, was hired for animated movies, one movie at a time. She felt, however, that the way her fiancé was treated was shocking. Her fiancé was hired project by project, film by film. If his skills were not useful for the next movie, he would simply lose his job. "How can you treat employees like that?" she asked me.

Well, I understood her. I come from Belgium, a country in which corporations are seen as families too. Japan is another country in which the culture of corporations is that of a family. When you start working for a company, you join a family. Your wage may be modest, but you get a car, and loads of benefits. Also, members of a family aren't fired, are they?

In the U.S., the typical corporate culture is not that of a family but of a guided missile.[1] Having a job means working on a project. Jobs are temporary. You work together on a project, and when the project is done, so is your job. You may or may not be invited for another project, but that depends on whether your skills are needed for that project. If not, then you simply move on to another job in another group, maybe in another city. No hard feelings.

---

[1]   Trompenaars and Hampden-Turner, *Riding the Waves of Culture: Understanding Diversity in Global Business* (McGraw-Hill, 2012).

17. Levmore's uniformity thesis

In 1986, University of Virginia Professor Saul Levmore traveled to Louisiana to participate in a conference on comparative law. Louisiana is the only U.S. state that has civil law, due to the fact that in 1804, when Louisiana became a part of the U.S., its citizens were predominantly of French descent. Law schools in Louisiana like to market themselves as offering a unique legal education—students receive a training in both civil and common law.

At the conference, however, Levmore argued that Louisiana law schools exaggerate the differences. Louisiana law can't be much different than Virginia law, Levmore reasoned, because law is a solution to problems and the problems are the same in all states. Levmore formulated the following thesis: in countries with the same development, law must be uniform unless the rules "(a) do not much matter or (b) raise issues about which reasonable people (even in the same culture) could disagree." (Levmore, Variety and Uniformity in the Treatment of the Good-Faith Purchaser (1987), Journal of Legal Studies, p. 44)

To illustrate, suppose someone asks you whether theft is allowed in Bolivia. While you don't know Bolivian law, you can be pretty sure that theft will be forbidden because theft would create the same problems as it would in the United States.

To illustrate the first exception, consider rules about what side of the road to drive at. In England, it is at the left side, in most other countries it is at the right side. There is no uniformity because it does not matter—both are equally fine as long as all car drivers stick to the same rule. As for the second exception, consider rules regarding marriage and divorce. What is the optimal divorce rule? Reasonable people can disagree about that.

There is a lot of variance among countries with respect to marriage and divorce law, but that is because we are not sure about optimal rules.

Levmore's thesis gives a theoretical explanation to an empirical finding of Aristotle more than 2,000 years earlier. Aristotle let his research assistants collect the laws of other city states and was amazed to see the degree of uniformity. He concluded that all legal systems have a common core, which he called "natural law" because these rules were apparently so logical that all city states adopted them.

In 1968, Schlesinger led a group of legal scholars from different legal families. The group used hypothetical cases and asked how these cases would have been solved in the different countries. Schlesinger and his colleagues found that the outcomes were very similar, although the concepts and doctrines to reach the outcomes differed significantly. This is consistent with the Levmore thesis: reasonable people can disagree about the most useful concepts and doctrines to use, even though they agree on the final result that needs to be reached.

Comparative lawyers have a tendency to exaggerate differences rather than similarities. One reason is that they often only look at the wording of the law, rather than at the result obtained by the law.

18. Old law is cheap law[1]

Rules may differ significantly if the countries are at a different stage of economic development. The relationship between legal rules and economic development is best understood using the "old law is cheap law" thesis.

Legal systems have expanded enormously over the centuries. The number of rules has grown exponentially—there are millions of rules right now. Similarly, the capacity of the legal system has grown—there are many more judges and lawyers than in the past.

The "old law is cheap law" theory holds that the growth of legal rules can best be understood by looking at the growth of the capacity.

A larger capacity changes the law in several ways. First, it allows the law to attack more types of undesirable behavior. When the legal system's capacity is limited, it can attack only the most harmful acts. As capacity grows, it can also attack acts that are less harmful at the margin.

Take precontractual liability—rules that deal with bad behavior during negotiations (before the contract is signed) that do not lead to a contract. An example is a window-dressing job interview with many candidates when the employer has already decided whom to hire. Although this act is socially harmful, its harm tends to be low—usually just the time lost by the candidates. In addition, adjudicating such cases is labor-intensive, as proving the employer's intentions and statements during negotiations is intrinsically difficult. Not surprisingly, no court on this planet accepted

---

[1]   This chapter draws heavily upon Gerrit De Geest, "Old Law Is Cheap Law", in Michael Faure, Wicher Schreuders and Louis Visscher (eds), *Don't Take It Seriously: Essays in Law and Economics in Honour of Roger Van den Bergh* (Cambridge, Intersentia 2018), 505–23.

precontractual liability cases before the 20th century. Although the doctrine was "invented" in the 19th century in Germany (by professor von Jhering), it was only in the 20th century that German courts started to apply it, soon followed by countries like the Netherlands, France and the U.S. Even today, precontractual liability is still underdeveloped.[2]

Secondly, a larger capacity allows courts to use rules that are better but require more work for the courts. Consider the strict, 17th-century version of the parol evidence rule. The rule held that whenever a contract was written on paper, no "parol evidence" (literally, "oral evidence", for instance testimony from witnesses) was allowed. A strict parol evidence rule is cheap law: courts only have to read within the "four corners" of the document. On the bright side, this allows courts to decide cases in 15 minutes, so to speak. On the not so bright side, this often leads to courts getting the facts wrong as the writing does not always reflect the true agreement.

In the 19th and 20th centuries, American courts carved out more and more exceptions. Today, parol evidence is permitted in a wide range of circumstances, for instance, when the document contains an error or looks incomplete. In some American states (the so-called "Corbin jurisdictions"), parol evidence is permitted even to contradict written terms. All these exceptions lead to higher-quality outcomes (courts are more likely to discover the truth), but they also require more work from the courts. Given capacity constraints, a strict parol evidence rule made sense in the 17th century.

"Old law is cheap law" means that in the past, when the economy was less developed, law was a product society spent less money on. Law was, in other words, a low-quality-low-price product. Just like low-income people buy a cheap house or a cheap car, poor societies buy cheap law. Cheap law is of lower quality in that it tolerates more harmful acts or leads to courts getting the facts wrong more often.

The "old law is cheap law" thesis explains *which* rules will be added or changed as capacity increases. In other words, its point is not that con-

---

2   See, for instance, Robert E. Scott, "*Hoffman v. Red Owl Stores* and the Myth of Precontractual Reliance" (2007) 68 Ohio State Law Journal 71 (arguing that American precontractual liability cases like *Hoffman* are outliers).

tract law (or any other field of law) has expanded since the 11th century. Its point is to explain *how* it has expanded, that is, to explain which rules were introduced first, and which were introduced later.

Why is this important for understanding your own legal system now? Legal systems often evolve toward a common point, but they rarely evolve at exactly the same time. Suppose the move goes from rule A to rule B. Eventually all legal systems will reach B. But at any moment of time, there are differences between countries and between American states. Some already have B while others still have A.

There is a danger that comparatists will overinterpret these differences, attributing them to cultural or economic differences, rather than to just coincidental delays in adaptation. Therefore, it is important to understand which rules change when countries become more developed.

Criminal law. Consider four types of harmful behavior: murder, rape, sexual harassment and bullying. While harm may vary in individual cases, people will likely agree that usually, murder is more harmful than rape, rape more harmful than harassment, and harassment more harmful than bullying. Therefore, expanding legal systems will criminalize these four types in that order.

Rules against murder are as old as the law. Rules against rape are old but not universally old[3] because the criminalization of rape happened later in some legal systems. For instance, in the old Roman Kingdom (753–509 BC), rape was not criminalized. This is illustrated by the event that led to the overthrow of the monarchy: the rape of Lucretia by one of the king's sons. The king's son defended himself by saying that there was no legal rule that dealt with rape. While the king's son did not violate

---

[3]   For instance, rape was a crime in Ancient Egypt. See James Bronson Reynolds, "Sex Morals and the Law in Ancient Egypt and Babylon" (2014) 5 Journal of the American Institute of Criminal Law and Criminology 20–31. Rape was also a crime under the code of Hammurabi, although the rape of a married woman was considered adultery so that both the rapist and the victim received the death penalty. Under Ancient Hebrew law, both rapist and the victim were executed under the assumption that the victim could have cried for help. Rape outside the city walls, in contrast, did not lead to a criminal but to a civil sanction—the rapist was required to marry the victim.

formal law, the citizens were so shocked that they revolted against the king and established the republic. Cicero later used this to illustrate that there is such a thing as natural law: the rapist should have known raping is wrong.[4] A different interpretation is that the rapist should have known this because he was violating social norms. As the Roman economy had become more developed, it was time to add rape to the list of offenses attacked by the legal system.

Sexual harassment became a legal wrong only in the 1970s.[5] Bullying had to wait until the 21st century. Indeed, between 1999 and 2015, all 50 American states have passed anti-bullying legislation; in some states, bullying is a crime. This illustrates that as the capacity of the legal system grows, it will start to attack marginally less harmful acts. Also, if your legal system has no anti-bullying legislation, it is probably only a matter of time, and not a matter of culture.

Tort law. Consider the evolution of tort liability from strict to negligence-based liability. Under strict liability, courts must check only whether there is harm and who caused it. (Liability is called strict because it does not depend on what the injurer was thinking.) If liability is negligence-based, courts must also check whether the injurer was negligent (or "at fault"). The latter demands more work, as it requires determining what is optimal care (which requires balancing care costs and expected accident costs) and what level of care the injurer exercised. Not surprisingly, old legal systems used strict liability. This is well-documented for tribal law. If a horse hit a pedestrian, the rider had to pay, even if he did nothing wrong. In Ancient Rome, strict liability was the normal rule until the Lex Aquilia (286 BC) introduced negligence-based liability.

Or consider the evolution from contributory negligence to comparative negligence in tort law in the 20th century. Contributory negligence means that, when both the injurer and the victim are negligent, the victim must bear the full loss (as she "contributed" to the accident). Comparative negligence means that, in such cases, both parties must bear a part of

---

4   Marcus Tullius Cicero (106–43 BCE) *De Legibus*, II, iv, 10.

5   *Barnes v. Train* (1974) is often cited as the first sexual harassment case under Title VII of the Civil Rights Act of 1964. Sexual harassment forms a crime in some cases, depending on state law (and often under the label of assault).

the loss, proportional to ("compared to") their culpability. Comparative negligence is considered fairer and it gives the two parties incentives to avoid the accident, but it requires extra work from the courts as they have to determine the relative culpability (50/50? 30/70?).[6] Not surprisingly, old law used contributory negligence. (The underlying moral justification was that one should not blame another if one is guilty himself; don't throw a stone if you have sins yourself. But this does not explain the later move to comparative negligence when Christian morality remained unchanged.) The switch to comparative negligence gradually happened in American states only in the 20th century, quickly followed by European countries.

Contract law: general evolution. Let us now look at how the English common law of contracts evolved.[7] In the early 12th century, courts didn't take any contract cases at all (only property and tort cases).[8] It would take until the 17th century until courts generally accepted contracts cases.

It is easy to explain why low-capacity courts may decide not to take contract cases. While contract breaches can be as harmful as torts or property violations, they are more subject to reputation sanctions. Reputation is indeed a strong mechanism in contracting, as contracts are voluntary transactions and most people who do trade do so repeatedly. Also, potential victims can protect themselves against contract breaches by demanding simultaneous performance (paying at the same time as delivering the good that is sold) or periodic payments (not waiting until the house has been completed but asking for several payments in between).

In the late 12th century, common law courts started to take one type of contract case—debts that had not been paid back.

---

[6]   For theoretical advantages of comparative negligence, see, e.g., Giuseppe Dari-Mattiacci and Gerritt De Geest, "The Filtering Effect of Sharing Rules" (2005) 34 Journal of Legal Studies 207–37. See also Michelle White, "An Empirical Test of the Comparative and Contributory Negligence Rules in Accident Law" (1989) 20 RAND J. of Economics 308–30 (suggestion that comparative negligence is more expensive to apply).

[7]   A concise history of the common law of contracts can be found in E. Allen Farnsworth, *Farnsworth on Contracts* (Aspen, 2003) §1.5–1.6.

[8]   Note that law merchant courts took contract cases in the medieval fairs and markets, and church courts enforced sworn promises, although this was prohibited in 1164.

Next, they also accepted refusals to pay for completed performance (for instance, a builder having finished a complete house and not being paid at all). At first glance, the potential loss for the victim is the same as under unpaid debt. Whether a $100,000 debt is not paid back, or the $100,000 price for a construction job is not paid, in both cases the promisee risks losing $100,000. In the second case, however, the potential victim can more easily protect herself by demanding instalments, for instance four instalments of $25,000 to be paid each time a fourth of the job is finished. (This increases transaction costs, but at least it reduces the vulnerability of the first to perform.) In the case of debt, no such protection is possible. Of course, the lender could not lend $100,000 but only $25,000 but that would defeat the purpose of the contract, which is to temporarily provide $100,000 capital.

From the early 15th century onwards, courts also accepted cases of defective performance. If the house was built and the $100,000 was paid, but later the house turned out to be defective, the victim could now go to court and demand compensation (technically, by extending tort law to "trespass on the case", which later became known as "assumpsit"). While defective performance can lead to significant losses, these losses are usually lower than the contract price. Moreover, determining to what extent performance was defective demands more of the courts' time than determining whether performance was complete. Therefore, the net benefit for allowing defective performance cases was likely lower than the net benefit for unpaid contract price cases.

By the second half of the 15th century, reliance damages could be awarded when a party hadn't even started performance. Reliance damages are harder to prove than damages caused by defective performance, and they are usually lower.

By the end of the 16th century (and especially since Slade's case in 1602), common law courts also accepted purely executory contracts (that is, contracts in which neither party had started performance). Here, the potential loss is only a foregone profit. The profit is nearly always smaller than the contract price. Moreover, it is harder for the court to know for sure that an agreement has been formed when performance hasn't even started. Therefore, the next benefit of this extension was lower than that of the three previous extensions.

It took until the 20th century, however, before precontractual liability was a ground for compensation in English courts. As explained earlier, it makes sense why no legal system intervened at the pre-contractual stage before the 20th century. The harm to the victim is usually modest, for instance lost time. Moreover, it is often hard for courts to find out who said what during negotiations, or what were the true motives of the parties. This does not mean that such strategies cause no social harm, but that expensive law is needed to correct this behavior.

Contract law: from formalism to mutual assent. Mutual assent seems like an obvious condition for a contract. Nonetheless, older legal systems, like old Roman law, didn't consider it a condition for the validity of a contract. Old Roman law was formalistic. A contract was formed when a ritual was undergone, in which certain words had to be uttered, and certain symbolic acts had to be performed (like the seller of land literally handing over some dirt of the land to the buyer). One implication was that there was a *numerus clausus* for contracts: only contracts for which such a ritual existed were legally valid. In late medieval times formalism was abandoned, the *numerus clausus* principle was given up, and the basic requirement for a contract became mutual assent.

Formalism can easily be seen as an example of "old law" that is "cheap law". Verifying whether certain rituals had been followed takes less time for the court than finding out whether there was a true meeting of minds.

Contract law: statutes of fraud and parol evidence. In the 17th century, when the majority of the population became literate, the English Statute of Frauds started to demand written evidence for many types of contracts. Combined with a strict parol evidence doctrine, this reduced the time courts needed to spend on contract cases. Courts only needed to quickly read the (usually short) document; they did not need to listen to witnesses or consider other information such as past transactions or customary practices.

Over time, as the courts' capacity increased, courts started to carve out exceptions to the Statute of Frauds. Anything that resembles a signature, such as a printed name on a form, is now fine. A few words on the back of a restaurant bill is enough. If one of the parties has started performance, the requirement for written evidence is dropped. Since the late 20th century, a name printed in an email serves as a valid signature.

All these relaxations of the Statute of Frauds resulted in higher-quality law—courts are more likely to find out what was truly agreed upon. At the same time, they mean more work for the courts. They are expensive law.

Contract law: economic duress instead of the pre-existing duty rule. Consider the facts of *Alaska Packers v. Domenico*. Fishermen were hired in San Francisco to sail to Alaska and work there for a cannery during the salmon season. When they arrived in Alaska, they refused to work unless they received $100 instead of the agreed-upon $50. The employer agreed because it was not possible to bring other workers over to Alaska before the end of the salmon season. Afterwards, the court decided that the employer had to pay only the originally agreed $50, not the $100.

There are two techniques to attack opportunistic renegotiations like this. The first is the consideration doctrine. The fishermen received more to do exactly the same as they had to do under the original contract; in other words, they had a pre-existing duty. Therefore, there was no rational motive ("consideration") for the employer's promise to pay more. As a result, the second promise was not binding, and the first contract was still governing.

The second technique is applying the economic duress doctrine. When courts take a careful look at the circumstances (analysing whether the "threat" was "improper" and whether the victim had a "reasonable alternative"), they may conclude that the second promise was induced under duress, and therefore is not binding.

The consideration doctrine is cheaper law. All the courts need to do is compare the two contracts. If the wage differs but not the amount of work, there is no consideration. Unfortunately, the consideration doctrine is easy to evade. If the fishermen had promised to work 15 minutes longer, they could have made the second contract valid, even if it was the outcome of an opportunistic renegotiation.

The economic duress doctrine is more expensive law because it requires an investigation into the circumstances of the renegotiation. But it can't be evaded by formalistic tricks like promising to work 15 minutes longer. It is expensive law, but better law, increasingly applied in the 20th century.

Contract law: from fraud (and caveat emptor) to far-reaching disclosure duties. In a perfect market there is no asymmetric information. In practice, that is often not the case. Better-informed parties have an incentive to keep information for themselves to exploit informational advantages. Better-informed parties may, therefore, flat-out lie, conceal information (deliberately make it harder for the other party to discover the truth), tell half-truths (which are literally true but still misleading because they suggest something untrue), or simply not disclose certain information.

Although the exploitation of asymmetric information may be socially harmful, attacking it is costly for the legal system. It takes time to investigate what statements have been made, whether these statements are false, whether the other party knew the same, and which party was in the best position to produce the information.

Old legal systems were governed by *caveat emptor*. *Caveat emptor* means literally that the buyer needs to beware. Although *caveat emptor* is sometimes interpreted as a legal rule that permits dishonesty, it can better be interpreted as the absence of a rule about honesty.[9]

As legal systems increased capacity, they started to carve out exceptions to *caveat emptor*. First, they prohibited plain fraud (cases in which words were said that were literally untrue). Then they attacked more subtle forms of fraud, such as concealment (cases in which no words were uttered) and half-truths (cases in which uttered words were misleading though not literally false). Later, they intervened whenever there was negligent misrepresentation (cases in which statements were carelessly made). Eventually, they developed far-reaching duties to disclose.

This chronological order makes sense. Fraud is likely the most harmful form of creating asymmetric information. After all, the lie is deliberately chosen to obtain the largest possible benefit to the maker of it (while the benefit of negligent misrepresentation to the maker is more like a lucky shot). Fraud is also harder to detect because it is deliberately constructed not to be detected. The only way victims can protect themselves against lies is to never believe any statement whatsoever made by the other party.

---

9   Walton H. Hamilton, "The Ancient Maxim Caveat Emptor" (1931) 40 Yale Law Journal 1113–87.

Within the fraud family, plain fraud involves the least work for the courts: courts have to check whether the statement was false, and whether the maker of the statement likely knew the falsehood. Concealment (like putting a pot of flowers on top of a wooden floor damaged by termites) requires more work for the courts, because it may be less obvious whether the concealer had the intent to mislead. Half-truths require even more work for courts, as the statements are literally true so that the court needs to examine the context in which they were made.

Negligent misrepresentation is highly complicated because it requires cost-benefit balancing—courts have to decide whether the factual mistake could have been corrected at reasonable costs. Duties to disclose involve even more balancing—whether information was worth being produced, which party was in the best position to produce it and whether the information was worth being communicated. Also, parties can protect themselves to some extent by asking questions (so that the other party's lack of a response may signal that he has something to hide, or so that the other party has to make a deliberate statement, which can be actionable if fraudulently made). In short, the "old law is cheap law" *thesis* can explain the gradual movement from fraud prohibitions to disclosure duties.

Contract law: from all-or-nothing incapacity to exploitation of irrationality. Old law worked with all-or-nothing rules: either someone had full capacity to make contracts or no capacity at all. Minors were categorically incapable of making contracts. If a merchant sold a good to a minor, there was no discussion—the parents could unwind the transaction. Drunken adults, on the other hand, were fully capable of entering contracts. Again, no discussion.

All-or-nothing rules make life easy for courts. All the courts have to check is the status of the plaintiff. Cheap law, however, is also low-quality law. It was impractical that minors could not participate in market transactions without their parents. It was also undesirable that drunken people could be exploited by letting them sign one-sided contracts.

Modern law has largely abandoned categorical thinking. Minors can enter into binding contracts for necessities at the normal price. In other words, minors can participate on the market, but adults cannot exploit their lack of experience by selling them goods they don't need or making them pay a higher price. Contracts can also be avoided if a non-drunken party exploited the drunkenness of the other party.

All these nuances mean more work for courts. Courts may have to examine the necessity of the goods, their market price, or the circumstances in which the transaction took place. Yet it is also higher-quality law, as the extra work prevents false negatives (denying binding force to good contracts) and false positives (enforcing exploitative contracts).

Contract law: the shrinking of definiteness requirements. Contracts are never complete. There are always unanticipated circumstances. If contracts are incomplete, courts may have to fill the gaps. Courts limit the amount of work they are willing to do, though, by requiring contracts to be sufficiently "definite". Originally, definiteness meant defining all major terms, such as the type of contract, price, quantity and quality. As the courts' capacity expanded over time, the definiteness requirement was relaxed. Section 2 of the UCC does not even require a price. All that the parties need to agree on is the type of good and the quantity. If no price is stipulated, courts will fill the gap by inserting the market price. Outside the UCC, courts sometimes do the same, especially in relational contracts (in which one party became vulnerable by making a relation-specific investment). In *Oglebay Norton v. Armco*, a transportation company had bought special vessels for a long-term contract with a steel factory. The contract stated a price formula for the duration of the contract. When a price index on which the formula was based disappeared, the court indicated it would determine the price if parties did not reach an agreement. More work for the courts, but better law.

Impossibility and impracticability. Consider the evolution from no excuses, to impossibility excuses, to impracticability excuses. In 1863, the highest English court created a major legal change in *Taylor v. Caldwell*. A concert hall had burned down, just before a concert series had to take place. The court decided that the owner of the hall didn't have to pay damages to the concert organizer, as the performance was excused because of impossibility. Since the concert organizer did not have to pay either, the decision let both parties share the loss, in that both lost their expected profit. Before this precedent, the owner would have had to pay damages to the concert organizer, which meant that the owner would have absorbed the entire loss (by losing not only his own profit but also by serving as the de facto profit insurer of the organizer's profit). *Taylor v. Caldwell* meant a better risk allocation, but also more work for the court in that the court had to determine whether performance had become impossible.

In the 20th century, impossibility was replaced by impracticability. Promisors are excused when the cost of performance greatly exceeds the value to the promisee, even if performance has not become literally impossible. Again, this is an even better risk allocation (by hedging the promisor's risk) but at the expense of even more work for the courts.

Contract law: mutual mistake. Mutual mistake means that both parties relied on the same, incorrect information. In the iconic case of *Sherwood v. Walker* (1887), a cow was sold for a low price, both parties believing the cow was barren. Before delivering the cow, however, the rancher discovered the cow was pregnant and worth ten times more. The court allowed rescission of the contract after asking a philosophical question: is a pregnant cow a different object than a non-pregnant cow? A century later, the highest court of the same state (Michigan) overruled the old, philosophical test and installed a new test that defines mutual mistake as a risk problem (*Lenawee County Board of Health v. Messerly* (1982)). The new test requires courts to ask how parties allocated this, or how rational parties would have allocated the risk.

The philosophical "what is a cow" test is cheap law. It takes only 15 minutes and a good cup of coffee to decide a case. Risk analysis requires a more difficult factual and empirical investigation but also leads to better risk allocation.

Contract law: self-help rules. Even developed legal systems cannot perfectly enforce all promises. Promisors may be insolvent, or damages may be hard to prove. Therefore, self-help rules remain important. One such rule is the right to withhold performance in response to the other party's breach (in civil law systems, this is better known under the Latin term *exceptio non adempleti contractus*.) Suppose that Preston promises to transfer his business to Kingston in return for money. If Kingston does not come up with security that the money will be paid, Preston may want to protect himself by postponing the transfer. This way, Kingston receives stronger incentives to get the deal financed, and Preston is better protected against Kingston's possible insolvency.

Before *Kingston v. Preston* (1773), English courts did not allow withholding performance. They considered all promises independent of each other. Preston had to deliver the business and Kingston had to provide security. If Kingston breached, that did not give Preston the right to breach. This was cheap law because courts did not have to look at the circumstances. All they had to do was check whether the defendant had kept his own promise. A right to withhold performance requires more work than a categorical "always do what you have literally promised" rule. Courts have to make sure that withholding performance is justified and not a cheap excuse to get out of an uninteresting deal.

Contract law: content regulation. Here, we can see a general evolution from relatively simple, specific rules (forbidding penalty clauses, forfeiture, covenants not to compete, or exemption terms) to standards (unconscionability, good faith). More court intervention, more circumstantial evidence, more types of bad behavior attacked, but more work for the courts.

Relevance for comparative law. One implication of the "old law is cheap law" theory for comparative law is that it warns us about overhasty cultural explanations. Often, differences exist because one country is still using cheap law when more expensive law makes sense. For instance, French courts were using, until recently, the impossibility criterion instead of the impracticability criterion. In 2005, the highest French court held that a contractor, who had built a house 33 cm lower than the height stipulated, could be forced to demolish the house and build a new one.[10] As explained, impracticability is better, but more expensive law. Given the fact that economic development is about the same in France as in the U.S. or Germany, there was no reason why only France was stuck in the old impossibility doctrine. And yes, in 2016, the new civil code moved to impracticability.[11] As it turns out, there was nothing inherently "cultural" about the use of impossibility in France. There is no reason why a modern, wealthy country should continue to use cheap law.

---

[10]   Cass. Civ. 11 May 2005, RTD Civ. 2005, 596 (Belhadji/Les Batisseurs du Grand Delta). See also Jan M. Smits and Caroline Calomme, *The Reform of the French Law of Obligations: Les Jeux Sont Faits* (2016). Maastricht European Private Law Institute Working Paper 2016-05.

[11]   Technically, the term "impracticability" is not used, though the criterion is implicitly applied under the heading of "imprévision" and limitations to specific performance. The new Article 1195 CC permits termination when an unforeseeable change of circumstances renders performance excessively onerous for a party. The new Article 1221 CC holds that specific performance cannot be asked if the costs would be clearly disproportionate to the benefits.

19. What jurisprudence books do American and European law professors prefer to read?

I have taught philosophy of law both in Europe and the U.S. (where it is called jurisprudence) and what surprised me most is how different the literature is. Indeed, European and American law professors read very different publications. You may think that this is normal because the law is also different. Yet we are not discussing positive law here, but fundamental research about law, which should transcend the details of a single legal system.

The dominant streams of American jurisprudence are normative philosophy (like Rawls or Nozick) and legal realism in all its forms (including Holmes, Llewellyn, critical legal studies, law and economics and new empirical legal realism). Legal realism has convincingly shown that law is never complete; there are always gaps that need to be filled and the choices that are made by judges who fill gaps are intrinsically political choices. Legal realism has also shown that legal reasoning that is presented as "pure logic" nearly always contains hidden premises that drive the results. And legal realism has proven over and over that judges do make legal rules, even when they pretend they don't.

Now, you would think that after so many years of American legal realism, French and German judges and law professors have changed their position. But that is not how human beings work. When they do not like the outcome of literature, they simply ignore that literature.

So, what do European continental lawyers read? Abstract theories that justify what they are doing. One strain of literature that has always been popular is analytical philosophy. (What is law? That is the type of questions European scholars are interested in. What is good law? Not so much.) Closely related to analytical philosophy, is the scholarship that Germans call *Begriffsjurisprudenz* ("concept philosophy"). In this scholarship, you try to help humanity by closing your eyes and thinking about the meaning of abstract concepts, such as "fault", "abuse of law" or "freedom of commerce". When I was a law student in Belgium, one of the "hot" issues was whether liability required a "light" fault or the "lightest fault". Article 1382 of the Napoleonic Civil Code (of 1804) uses the term "fault" but does not define it. Some scholars argued that a light fault had to be the norm, because we want people to be careful, but we do not expect them to act like Superman. Others argued that the lightest fault had to be the norm, because committing a fault is crossing a line, and even the lightest fault crosses the line. At that time, I did not fully understand the discussion, and so many years later I still don't find it a productive approach. The American approach is much more useful here: just ask what the social problem is that you want to solve. Do we want fewer accidents or less pollution? Let's then study which legal rules have that effect. But this sounds too political to German ears. And from a French perspective, it is too threatening, because it reveals that courts do more than just interpret the law.

One of the scholars who had an enormous impact in Europe but hardly any in the U.S. is the Austrian scholar Hans Kelsen. Kelsen's work is quite abstract (you may recognize the German tradition here!), but let me try to summarize it in a few lines. According to Kelsen, the question is not whether law is just or fair or effective or economically optimal, but whether it is "valid". A legal rule is valid when it is ultimately in accordance with the highest legal norm (the *Grundnorm*). Suppose you receive a parking fine and ask whether the city has the right to write such tickets (that is, you ask whether the city ordinance on which your fine is based is "valid"). Well, maybe they have this right according to a higher legislative Act that gave them this authority. But is that Act valid? Yes, if it was approved after the procedure described in the current constitution. But is the current constitution valid? Yes, if all the changes since the first constitution were made according to the procedure described in the first constitution, according to the procedure described in later amendments that were approved according to the original constitution, or according to later valid versions. But is the first constitution valid? Well, that is an axiom that you have to accept, according to Kelsen. If you do not accept that, you should not become a lawyer!

Now, you immediately see why European lawyers love Kelsen. They do not have to ask whether the law is fair or effective, but only whether the law is the law. They can remain apolitical, neutral lawyers, who apparently just apply the rules approved by the top of the legal organization. Moreover, they can still criticize the law (which they like to do), as long as they frame their critique in terms of "logic" and "consistency". It seems as if the legal realists have trashed the foundations on which Kelsen's theory is based, but that is no problem, because European lawyers choose not to read legal realism.

Are there any common law scholars whose writings continental Europeans like? Well, there are a few, and one of them is Ronald Dworkin. The starting point of Dworkin is that law consists not only of rules, but also of principles. This sounds obvious, but Dworkin uses this as a starting point to argue that courts can fill gaps in the law without making new law. How can they ever do that? Well, when courts make a new precedent, they do not make new law, according to Dworkin, but they just apply existing general principles, and hence apply existing law. So in "hard cases" (in which the law does not seem to give an immediate answer, because there is basically a gap in the law), judges look for "the right answer", through an "interpretative approach" (which involves respect for past governmental actions like legislation and precedents). Hence, in hard cases, no new law is made, but existing law is applied, according to Dworkin.

Dworkin's viewpoint has many aspects, but let's just illustrate its fundamental absurdity by applying it not to judges but to other entities who make legal rules: parliaments and presidents. When they make new laws, they could also argue that they just apply some general principles of law. But imagine a president or senator who would argue something along the following lines in a re-election campaign: "I did not make any policy decision during the last four years. I just wrote down the law that was already there." Nobody would find this convincing. So why would it be more convincing if a judge tried the same camouflage trick?

It should be no surprise that Dworkin has great difficulties convincing American law professors of the correctness of his viewpoint. So why is his work so well-received in European civil law countries? Because he writes what they like to hear. Judges who never make new rules, and never take political positions ... law professors who can make proposals for filling gaps in the law, solely based on existing principles of law ... exactly what they love to hear in France and Germany!

How about the most successful variant of American legal realism—law and economics? Well, there is some interest in Europe from politicians and public administrations who are openly in the business of preparing policy. There is also some interest in economics departments, because economists have come to realize that institutions matter. But continental European law schools? Much less. The open argumentation of law and economics is simply too much for the French, with their centuries-long tradition of presenting case law as pure interpretations of codified law. And economic evaluation of legal rules is simply too much for the German legal culture with its deeply rooted fear of statements that involve a political or ethical position. Law and economics will always have a more difficult life in European civil law systems than analytical philosophy and legal theory (which can deliver inspiration for *Begriffsjurisprudenz*, and which is too abstract to be seen as a political threat) and legal history (which can inspire new "interpretations" of the law).

You may believe that at the end of the day, every scholarship is a matter of taste, and that all tastes are equally good. But unfortunately, this is not so. What is the best remedy for contract breach? To what extent is it desirable to hold parties liable at the precontractual stage? When should strict liability be used instead of negligence? What corporate law rules are needed to reduce self-dealing? Those are the type of research questions that need to be answered if you want to improve the quality of your legal system. Yet, to such questions you will not find an answer in the European legal literature. The European literature will tell you what the law is, not what good law is. But a legal system that does not let its scholars reflect on good law is unlikely to produce good law.

PART III

Substantive legal differences

20. Constitutional law

No country on earth seems to spend a larger share of its GDP on constitutional law scholarship than the U.S. More American professors write on constitutional law than seems to be justified by its practical importance. And those constitutional scholars do not write short articles; they write long essays and thick books. Similarly, American law schools offer more constitutional law courses than is the case in any other country. Constitutional law is a mandatory course at nearly all law schools.

For one part this is a good thing. American constitutional law is "thicker" than constitutional law in most other countries because of its thicker civil rights section. Civil rights are rights of citizens towards the government. These constitutional rights put constraints on governments; without such constraints, governments may overreach. Therefore, a society with many such constraints on the government, like the U.S., may be a better society.

In recent decades, civil law countries have somewhat closed the gap though. Many have non-discrimination and equality terms in their constitution now. Many have constitutional courts that are allowed to check whether legislation is consistent with the constitution.

However, civil rights alone cannot explain why American constitutional scholarship is such an outlier. There is more to it. Constitutional discussions fascinate American professors. Put a constitutional law professor, a contract law professor, a criminal law professor and a tax law professor together at a dinner table and they will end up debating constitutional cases.

That is very different in civil law countries where constitutional law is just one of the many fields of law—not a special field but just a field. Sure, constitutional scholars in civil law countries write comments on recent decisions and some write textbooks that summarize constitutional law. But they don't write dozens of books offering grand theories on yet another life-threatening aspect of the constitution. And constitutional law does not trigger endless discussions among professors of different fields.

Why are American professors so fascinated in constitutional cases? Here is my own little theory: they are fascinated because American constitutional law is in a sense un-American. American constitutional law is, at its core, a civil law tradition within a common law country.

Here is why. As we have seen, the main difference between common law and civil law is that common law judges dare to openly make new rules. They can say, for instance, "My name is Judge Learned Hand and here is a formula I have just made up." Civil law judges make new rules too, but they nearly always deny it. They do not say, "There was no rule or the rule was bad and so I made this new rule." Instead they say, "I am only applying the Civil Code, and I discovered this rule by reading Article 1382 over and over again. It was hidden there for over 200 years until I found it."

Alternatively, common law judges openly reveal the policy reasons for their decisions. By contrast, civil law judges hardly ever reveal why they preferred one rule over another. As a matter of fact, they can't reveal these policy reasons because that would reveal that they are making policy. Civil law scholars have a distaste for policy discussions. They act as if they are neutral observers, or value-neutral "legal scientists".

The U.S. is the ultimate common law country. More so than in England, American judges dare to openly make new rules. American judges extensively discuss the advantages and disadvantages of legal rules. They explain why they believe that one rule is better than another rule.

Amazingly, the United States Supreme Court acts more like a civil law court than as a common law court. U.S. Supreme Court judges do not openly admit that the U.S. Constitution is incomplete or outdated; they do not openly admit that many constitutional rules are made up by the judges. Instead, they act as if they all read it in certain words of the Constitution. Of course, they have not read this in those words. But they cannot openly admit that, because they are officially only allowed to apply the Constitution, not to *write* the Constitution. And so they behave like civil law judges. They first make the rules and then go through constitutional texts until they find a sentence in which they can read what they have already decided.

Amazingly, many American constitutional scholars try to do the same thing. But in a sense this is not so amazing—European civil law scholars do the same.

The result is that American constitutional law is continuously expanding according to unarticulated principles. And the choice of the new principles is not always logical. For instance, suppose that I say that driving carelessly should be considered a constitutional violation. Constitutional scholars will reply that I can't read that in the Constitution. And they are right. The founding fathers did not think about driving carefully when they wrote the Constitution. But suppose you argue that your neighbor, Peeping Tom, is violating your constitutional right of privacy by peeping over the hedge. The right of privacy is read in the "due process" words of the 14th Amendment:

> 14th Amendment, 1. All persons born or naturalized in the United States, and subject to the jurisdiction thereof, are citizens of the United States and of the State wherein they reside. No State shall make or enforce any law which shall abridge the privileges or immunities of citizens of the United States; nor shall any State deprive any person of life, liberty, or property, *without due process of law*; nor deny to any person within its jurisdiction the equal protection of the laws. …

Let's face it: the right of privacy is not in the 14th Amendment. The founding fathers did not think for a second about Peeping Tom.

So, there must be an invisible criterion that determines which fantasies can be elevated to constitutional rights and which can't. But when I ask about that invisible criterion, my constitutional law colleagues don't want to discuss it. They may say that it's a "living constitution" but if it lives, why can't it move my way? They may say that it is a matter of what the Supreme Court decided so far, but if whatever the Supreme Court decides is constitutional law, how can they criticize the Supreme Court for not choosing the right answer?

My guess is that this schizophrenia is what drives all this attention to constitutional law. Common law scholars intuitively feel there is something odd about all those constitutional law debates. Common law scholars are used to fully open discussions. They are not used to discussions in which some of the criterions for valid arguments are not revealed.

Common law and civil law are very different types of approaches. Common law is based on open argumentation, civil law on closed argumentation. So if you look at this planet, where exactly does the battle take place, location-wise? Maybe you thought it was in the European Union, where England, France, and Germany were trying to build a common legal system. Or maybe in Louisiana or Quebec, two civil law states in common law countries. But I am becoming more and more convinced that the real battle takes place in American constitutional law. A system of closed argumentation within a system of openness. A civil law island within a common law sea.

21. Criminal law and criminal procedure

Plea bargaining. A plea bargain in a criminal case is the equivalent of a settlement in a civil case. The defendant agrees to plead guilty, so that a lengthy and expensive trial can be avoided. In return, the prosecutor agrees to lower the charge. For instance, the accused risks a 20-year sentence after a trial and the prosecutor makes a deal for only 10 years in jail. Both parties are better off, or so goes the argument. The accused has to serve less time in prison, and the prosecutor has the certainty of having another criminal put behind bars and the benefit of having to devote less time on this one case.

The plea bargain agreement has to be approved by the court (in a much shorter procedure). The court has to confirm that the defendant is well-informed, and that the guilty plea has a factual basis.

Plea bargaining fits well within the adversarial philosophy: prosecutors are free to decide whether they prosecute and on what charge they will prosecute. Defendants are free to avoid the costs and embarrassment of a trial by pleading guilty. If the two parties agree that they will not fight it out, that agreement should be binding.

In the U.S., the vast majority of convictions (over 90%) are obtained on guilty pleas. The U.S. Supreme Court said in 1971 that plea bargaining is an essential component to the administration of justice. Without it, the number of judges would need to be multiplied. For instance, Germany has three times more judges than the U.S.

Implicit forms of plea bargaining in civil law countries. While plain forms of plea bargaining are typically not allowed in civil law countries (aside from Italy, where it has been introduced as a tool in the war against the mafia since 1989), there are some implicit forms that are permissible.

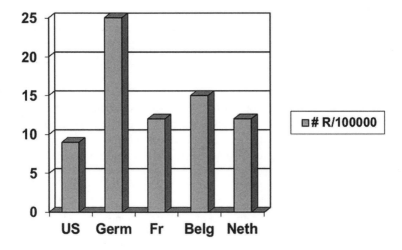

Figure 21.1   Number of judges per 100,000 inhabitants

For instance, in France and Belgium prosecutors can promise to reduce the charge so that a lower court (the Correctional Court) decides instead of a jury in the Court of Assize. If defendants choose not to contest the charges, the procedure can be as brief as the American procedure in which the guilty plea is taken. Another technique in civil law countries is using "administrative fines": for minor offences, prosecutors may promise not to prosecute if an administrative fine is voluntarily paid. This is used in many civil law countries for traffic fines.

Compulsory prosecution in civil law countries. Why is plea bargaining not allowed in civil law countries? Because it is seen as a procedure that gives too much discretion to the prosecutors and too little to the judges. Civil law is often said to be characterized by the denial of discretion to the prosecutor. Historically there was even "compulsory prosecution": prosecutors were obliged to bring each case to court, even if they were convinced that the defendant was innocent or that there was insufficient evidence to convict the defendant. Compulsory prosecution is now largely (though not completely) abolished because it was seen as too time consuming. But the underlying philosophy still lives—that it is not up to the prosecutor but up to the court to decide the case.

The defendant's incentives to speak and perjury. Civil law countries usually put more pressure on defendants to testify (Langbein, 1979). In a well-reported case involving a Belgian soccer coach accepting bribes, the nicotine-addicted coach started to give information 12 hours after he was denied cigarettes. In civil law countries, there is no formal right to be silent.

On the other hand, suspects cannot be heard under oath. As a result, they cannot commit perjury. This gives them an incentive to come up with their own version of the story. (Note that this rule is sometimes circumvented by first hearing future defendants as witnesses because they can be interrogated under oath.)

In the U.S., defendants have the right to remain silent. This follows from the rule against self-incrimination of the Fifth Amendment, which states:

> No person shall be held to answer for a capital, or otherwise infamous crime, unless on a presentment or indictment of a Grand Jury, except in cases arising in the land or naval forces, or in the Militia, when in actual service in time of War or public danger; nor shall any person be subject for the same offense to be twice put in jeopardy of life or limb; nor shall be compelled *in any criminal case to be a witness against himself* ...

This silence may not be interpreted as an implicit confession of guilt. In civil law countries, on the other hand, the fact that the defendant does not speak can be considered (by the court or the jury) as additional evidence of guilt.

Why these differences? The American philosophy is that the government is intrinsically more wealthy and powerful than an individual citizen. To level the playing-field, defendants need to be given more rights, including the right to not testify at all. Also, the universalist American culture has little tolerance for lying, while the particularist culture in countries like France, has a higher tolerance for lying, although it can tolerate less that people remain silent.

In 1989 an American military airplane tried to fly under the cables of a cable car in the ski station Cavalesi. Unfortunately, the plane did not fly low enough so that wires were cut with its tail. The cable car fell down and 20 people died. Shortly after the accident, the American pilots were arrested and asked in front of cameras what had happened. They replied they wanted to remain silent. The Europeans were shocked. If the pilots had come up with a false story, that would have been less shocking. In the U.S., in contrast, coming up with a false statement is highly problematic, and interrogation is even done under oath.

Gun control. The right to bear weapons is a constitutionally protected right. Although the wording of the Second Amendment is confusing, its interpretation is generally accepted not to mean the right to form militias, but the right for individuals to protect themselves using weapons.

In most European countries, a license to use a weapon requires a serious administrative procedure. Still, the difference in the use of weapons is not so much a matter of law but of culture. Europeans and Asians are scared of weapons.

Where does the American love for guns come from? The early settlers had farms with lots of land. They lived at large distances from each other. Before the invention of the car and the phone, they lived hours away from the police. So, when they were robbed they had to defend themselves. They could not rely on the police, not because the police were lazy but because the police were too far away. Not surprisingly, most strong proponents of guns live in rural areas. The strongest opponents live in crowded cities. A similar pattern can be seen in Europe, where the possession of firearms is the highest in sparsely populated Northern states like Finland.

Higher incarceration rate. Per capita, the U.S. has 10 times more people in jail than Germany and 20 times more than in the Netherlands. What explains this perplexing difference?

For starters, fewer inmates get parole in the U.S. In the French tradition, nearly all inmates get parole after one third of the sentence. The difference in attitude towards parole may be correlated with Catholicism, where you can confess and receive forgiveness of your sins at any time in your life, versus Protestantism, where only God can forgive you if you have done enough in your life to outweigh the sins.

Secondly, sentences tend to be higher because of the Sentencing Guidelines. These often create high minimum sanctions. If you think about it, these guidelines are more in the civil law style than common law style. There are top-down directions, authorized by an Act of Congress, to reduce the decision freedom of the courts.

Thirdly, many more people in American prisons are convicted for drug-related crimes. The Netherlands, on the other hand, has a softer, more tolerating attitude towards drugs.

Fourthly, the arm's length relationship between prosecutor and defendant plays a role. Suppose that a prosecutor believes that five years of jail is a fair sanction. In civil law countries, the prosecutor will demand five years. In the U.S., the prosecutor will demand 10 years and consider it a victory if more than five years are given. This system could work if it is truly an arm's length battle, with a suspect who has the same financial resources as the government. In practice, it is an unequal battle.

That being said, I have never met an American professor of criminal law who believes that the current mass incarceration is a good thing. The question, then, is why a system that is considered wrong isn't changed. This brings us to the last explanation.

Democracy. Maybe it is because the U.S. is more democratic than most European countries. In the U.S., many judges need to get elected or reelected. Many prosecutors later go on to become politicians and usually their selling point is that they are "tough on crime". (I have never seen a TV commercial in which a political candidate bragged he had been soft on crime.) By contrast, in most European countries, criminal policy is not on the political agenda. The death penalty was abolished by a treaty, the European Convention on Human Rights (and more specifically Protocol 6).

In the U.S., the death penalty is still applied in about half of the states. My guess is that if there was a vote on the death penalty, half of the European countries would apply the death penalty as well. By the same token, democracies tend to lead to more severe sentencing, partly because inmates have no voting rights, and partly because the crimes committed by released criminals (type 1 errors) are more salient in newspapers than criminals serving too long sentences (type 2 errors).

22. Civil procedure

The largest differences among legal systems can be found in the field of civil procedure. Two characteristics drive the differences: the adversarial style of litigation and the broad use the U.S. makes of juries.

Adversarial trials. An adversarial trial is a trial led by the parties, not by the judge. The judge watches but rarely intervenes. If parties devote too much energy arguing about an unimportant issue, the judge will not stop them. If they devote too little energy to a major point, or even overlook a major legal point, the judge will not intervene.

Is an adversarial trial better or worse than an inquisitorial trial? Dewatripont and Tirole (1999), two economists specialized in industrial organization, start their analysis by pointing at the fact that the adversarial trial leads to duplicative work. What is the task of the advocate of party A? To check the law and check the facts. What is the task of the advocate of party B? To check the law and check the facts. What is the task of the judge? To check the law and check the facts. Instead of hiring advocates, why don't the parties go directly to the judge, who will check the law and check the facts?

The reason, according to Dewatripont and Tirole, is that an inquisitorial system does not give enough incentives to a judge to thoroughly check the law and the facts. A judge could pretend to have worked eight hours on a case, while in reality she spent 15 minutes on the case and the other seven hours and 45 minutes at a golf course. Can't advocates do the same? In theory they can, but if the other advocate works eight hours effectively, the golf playing advocate will lose most cases and will quickly run out of clients. An adversarial system creates strong incentives for advocates to work hard. It is a battle in which both have strong incentives to fight hard.

How can civil law systems overcome the problem of the golf playing judge? By monitoring the judge, who is less independent and more a part of a large organization. Also, an appellate procedure does everything over from scratch but this times with three judges. If the judge at the first instance devoted too little effort to the case, that will be discovered.

Jury system as a theater play. The U.S. uses juries for most civil trials. How does that change the rules of procedure? A trial is like a theater play—on the day of the premiere everything needs to be ready because the show must go on. If new evidence would be presented, the other party can't say, "Please give me a week to study this." Juries can't be sent home and be brought back one week later. Professional judges, on the other hand, are flexible. They can come back a week later.

Discovery. American trials start with discovery. The rule is that all parties exchange all evidence they have and that evidence that was not shown at this early stage cannot be shown at a later stage. Most other countries don't have a formal discovery stage. The American jury system makes it necessary to have a discovery stage because lawyers must be prepared on all possible factual arguments once the jury trial starts. The next stage is the pretrial stage, in which parties and the judge determine what evidence may be presented at the trial in front of the jury. The final stage is the jury trial itself. This differs from most civil law countries where new evidence can be brought in at any stage, even for the first time in appeal. Civil law countries don't have a strict discovery and pretrial stage.

Fishing expeditions. Sometimes, the plaintiff asks the defendant for a gigantic number of documents during discovery. For instance, "Give me a printout of all internal emails of a whole year of that department in your company." This is called a fishing expedition, where the plaintiff is allowed to fish in the ocean, hoping to catch a certain type of fish. Fishing, in other words, is looking for evidence that has a chance to be relevant, without knowing beforehand how it could be relevant. Some see this as an abuse of the discovery rights. This is certainly the view in civil law countries, where fishing expeditions are not allowed. Others see this as an indispensable method of collecting evidence. What drives the difference? The American culture of extreme honesty. In this culture, the truth must be discovered at any cost.

Neutral versus biased expert witnesses. In Germany and France, the court appoints the expert witness (typically one only). This expert witness tries to be as neutral as possible, in order to please the court and get more work later. In the U.S., each party hires her own expert witness. So, expert witnesses are biased. They look at the reality from one side, in order to get more jobs in the future. In a sense, American expert witnesses are specialized advocates. For instance, they have training in statistics and can analyse data better than the main advocates.

German system: judges play an active role. By contrast, trial is more inquisitorial in Germany. The court leads the evidence taking. The court decides which evidence it will use, which documents it wants to see, and which witnesses it wants to hear. Also, the court interrogates the witnesses. In the U.S., in contrast, the lawyers of the parties are the ones interrogating the witnesses. Lawyers also prepare the witnesses beforehand. In Germany, talking to witnesses outside the courtroom is considered unethical. The German judge is also the manager of the procedure (for instance, she will bundle the hearing of several witnesses).

German judges have to think out loud. They have a duty to inform the parties of the evidence and legal arguments that they consider important. If one of the attorneys makes an error, the judge has to give a hint. The only limit is that the judge should avoid appearing biased. In practice, German judges can make the attorneys work harder (when the major issues have been overlooked until that point) or work less hard (when energy is devoted to issues that are not decisive).

See Section 139 of the German Code of Civil Procedure:

(1) The presiding judge shall make sure that the parties make full statements about all material facts and make appropriate motions, *especially to elaborate on insufficient statements* regarding the facts and to indicate the means of proof. Therefore, if necessary, *he shall discuss the factual and legal issues of the case* and issues with the parties and ask questions.

(2) The presiding judge shall bring to the parties' attention *doubts that the court has* because of its duty to take certain points into account on its own motion.

(3) He shall permit each member of the court to ask such questions as that member requests. [Italics added]

Why don't American judges think out loud? Some do, by asking questions, especially at the appellate stage. But trial judges can't think out loud because the judgment is made by the jury, and the trial judge can't predict what the jury members will consider important.

Lawyer's fees. Theoretically, there are three ways to pay lawyers. First, lawyers can be paid at an hourly rate. This is the most common arrangement on the planet. It gives an incentive to the client not to waste the lawyer's time, although it may give the lawyer an incentive to devote more hours than needed, for instance by recommending not to accept a settlement proposal and by litigating instead.

Secondly, lawyers can receive a fixed fee per case. This is the common arrangement in Germany. The reason is related to the loser-pays-all system in Germany. The loser has to pay the reasonable advocate's cost of the other party, but what is reasonable? Tables with official fees are defined, and, in practice, they have received a fixed fee character. Also, charging less than the official fees is considered unethical in Germany. The result is that most litigators work for the official fees. Fixed fees give incentives to work fast, but they may give an incentive to work faster than is optimal.

Thirdly, lawyers may receive contingent fees. These are fees contingent upon the outcome. Contingent fees mean that the lawyer is only paid when the case is won. Percentages vary between 5% and 33%, depending on the type and difficulty of the case. The lawyer bears 100% of the costs if the case is lost and receives a part of the amount-at-stake if the case is won.

Contingent fees are frequently used in the U.S., but are forbidden in most European countries, outside of a few exceptions. Why are they forbidden? They are believed to give too strong an incentive to lawyers to win a case. But isn't that the goal—that the one who works for you fights nearly as hard as if it was for herself? Also, contingent fees are a great alternative for low-income clients, who can't afford to pay the bill when the case is lost. In most European countries, low-income parties can get free (i.e., subsidized) legal aid. This is less so in the U.S.

Should the loser pay all? In principle, parties bear their own lawyer's costs in the U.S., although the loser does pay the court costs. In Europe, including England, the dominant rule is that the loser pays all costs.

But how much is paid in practice? In most European countries, the compensation is undercompensatory. The only country that gives 100% compensation is Germany. On the other hand, there are hundreds of statutes in the U.S. that shift the winner's fee to the loser. Some of these are asymmetric. For instance, consumer protection legislation typically lets the business pay the costs as a loser, but not the consumer. If we take all fee-shifting statutes into account, there may be more fee shifting in the U.S. than in many European countries.

Which rule is better? The German rule is better at discouraging opportunistic refusals to pay, especially for low amounts. Suppose I owe you $100 and I refuse to pay you. In the U.S., you will lose money if you bring me to court, even if you win. Indeed, your lawyer costs will be higher than $100. In Germany, you may bring me to court because all lawyers' costs will have to be paid by the loser—me.

On the other hand, the American rule avoids having to draft official fees. Also, the rule implicitly subsidizes parties who start risky cases in the hope of creating a new precedent. This is important for a legal system that largely relies on precedents.

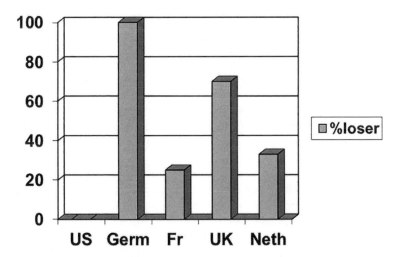

Figure 22.1   Percentage of costs paid by the loser of the trial

In civil law countries, class actions are in principle not allowed. Class actions are court procedures in which the lawyer does not represent just one client but a whole group of clients. Class actions are important when many victims suffer a small loss. Suppose that a company wrongfully overcharges one million customers $30 each. Nobody would sue for $30. But a million times $30 is $30 million—an amount worth suing for. Class actions permit attorneys to sue on behalf of the entire class of one million victims.

Class actions are common in the U.S. but forbidden (aside from a few exceptions) in the rest of the world. How do these countries solve the problem of stealing $30 from a million people? They solve it through public (criminal) law. The practice is defined as a crime, and the prosecutor goes after the wrongdoer.

The U.S. has an attorney-general who can often do the same. Still, attorney-generals have insufficient capacity to go after all violations.

Businesses don't like class actions, though, and many make them impossible through contractual arbitration terms to an arbitration court that does not do class actions. For tort law, they are still widespread because tort actions are usually among "strangers" who haven't met each other before the accident and who are therefore not bound by contractual arbitration terms.

Why is there such a high settlement rate in the U.S.? The overwhelming majority of American cases are settled out of court. It is hard to know the real number, since many are settled even before suit is initiated in court. Still, 95%–99% is a number often heard. In France and Germany, the number of settlements is clearly below 50%. How can we explain this large difference?

Theoretical models say that parties will settle when they can well predict what the court will decide. Trial only happens when at least one of the parties has an unrealistically rosy view on who will win.

American law is the best-developed law. There are an enormous number of published precedents. There are numerous law professors who write numerous books and articles. Nearly every question has already been answered. Also, dissenting opinions are published, making the view of the current judge more predictable. All these factors make the court decision more predictable and, therefore, settlement more likely.

In the U.S., cases are often settled after discovery. Since both lawyers can see all the evidence, they can better predict who will win. Since they are both professionals, they have realistic expectations. It is better to settle "in the shadow of the law" than to waste time and money to obtain the same result.

The way lawyers are paid plays a role as well. Contingent fees give the lawyers strong incentives to settle: it is more economical for them to receive money for less work than when the court goes to trial. Hourly fees, on the other hand, give lawyers an incentive to make more hours and therefore to push less for settlement.

Another factor is how costly litigation is. If litigation is costly, settling becomes more cost saving. If litigation is cheap, there is less urgency to settle. Since litigation is cheaper in France and Germany than in the U.S., this is another explanation for why settlement rates are higher in the U.S.

Why were settlement rates so high in traditional Japan? First, there were precise and predictable rules. Secondly, there weren't many lawyers, which made legal fees sky-high. Thirdly, courts were expensive. Fourthly, there were cultural norms that disapproved of litigating. The predictability of the outcome combined with the costliness of trial (both financially and morally) leads to a high rate of settlements.

Process duration. Let us now look at some general performance measures, starting with process duration.

U.S. courts are fast, but not extremely fast. German courts are faster. Why? First, judges can take the lead more in Germany. Secondly, there are many judges pro capita in Germany. Thirdly, advocates have an incentive not to waste too much time with unimportant issues because they are paid a fixed fee. In the U.S., the whole process is more perfectionist: the truth has to be discovered at all costs.

USA: is too much spent on litigation? In the U.S., when cases are not settled, the legal expenses are among the highest. Sometimes it is said that it takes a dollar to get a dollar. The more that will be spent, the higher the

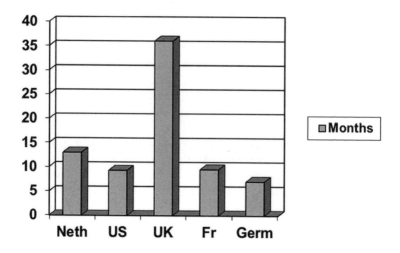

Figure 22.2   Average process duration (in months)

chance that courts will find out the (legal and factual) truth, and the more credible a threat to go to trial will be, and so the higher the enforcement factor will be.

When we balance trial expenses on the one hand and enforcement improvement gains on the other hand, are current litigation expenses optimal in the U.S.? One economic argument holds that an expensive, perfectionist trial is better than a mistake-making cheap trial. Suppose that in the U.S. 99% of the cases are settled, so that only 1 in 100 go to trial. Suppose also, at an earlier stage, that most people simply follow the rules so that there is only a conflict in 1% of the cases because 99% of the population complies with the rules. Multiply both and you will find that out of 10,000 situations only one goes to trial. Economically it is way more important that most of the 10,000 people comply with the law than that the one trial is cheap. (Geoffrey Miller, 1997).

There are also data that suggest that common law countries have a higher economic growth and a higher enforcement of property and contract rights, and that the two may be causally linked (Mahoney, 2001). So, American litigation may be expensive, but it works like a stick that makes most people comply with it or settle out of court.

French procedural law leads to lower quality but cheaper procedures (for instance, relying on written evidence simplifies the procedure, but the exclusion of other valuable sources of evidence reduces the chance that the court will find out the truth). As a result, property and contract rights are less enforced (as courts make more errors). The common law produces faster economic growth through greater security of property and contract rights.

No precedent without a case? China is different. As we have seen, a large part of the law is judge-made in the U.S. Building up such a stockpile of cases takes time. What can developing countries do to catch up fast?

The Chinese Supreme Court published a book on the interpretation of the contract law code. It says what the court would decide if a case was filed! In the eyes of many, this is a doubtful strategy to create precedents, but on the bright side, this is an efficient way to develop the law fast. Do Chinese judges of the Supreme Court have time for that? Yes, because there are 700 judges in the Supreme Court! This is many more than the nine judges in the U.S. Supreme Court.

23. Evidence

Evidence is a major course at American law schools. Most students take it. The rules of evidence have to be known at the bar exam. That is different from civil law countries. For instance, the Napoleonic Code of 1804 devoted only a few pages to evidence rules. (When I studied law in Belgium, evidence wasn't even an optional course. Now, it is an optional course in civil law countries, but few students take it.)

Why the difference? It's all about juries. Members of juries are no professionals. They are easy to mislead. Therefore, there must be detailed rules about what evidence can be presented to them. For instance, there is a strict rule against hearsay evidence, since jury members may attach too much weight to it.

In civil law countries, by contrast, there are usually no juries (and definitely not for non-criminal cases). Professional judges are professionals. You can present any evidence that you think can convince them, but at the same time you realize that they are hard to manipulate.

Also, there is more awareness of the evidence standards for the different law fields in the U.S. Consider the OJ Simpson case. OJ Simpson was a former football player who was accused of having murdered his wife and her friend. The entirety of America followed the criminal trial in the media. To everybody's surprise, OJ was found not guilty for murder. His wife's relatives sued him then for tort in a different court. This time, OJ Simpson lost. So, he had to pay damages to his wife's family for having murdered his wife. Many outside the U.S. felt that the legal system was inconsistent here. Yet from an evidence point of view, that is not necessarily the case. The burden of proof in a criminal trial is "proof beyond reasonable doubt". Although it is hard to put a percentage on this, one number sometimes heard is 95% certainty. The burden of proof in a tort case is preponderance of evidence, which is 51% because it means that one hypothesis is slightly more plausible than another hypothesis. If there was an 80% chance that OJ Simpson was guilty, he should indeed have been found not guilty in the criminal trial (because 80% < 95%) but guilty in the civil trial (because 80% > 51%).

In France, the criminal and tort aspects would have been judged in one single trial. This means that, in practice, the same high evidence burden is required for both criminal and tort liability, which is not logical. But in France, less attention is paid to evidence rules than in the U.S.

24. Administrative law is much thinner in the U.S.

The concentration of power in civil law countries leads to other surprising consequences. One is that administrative law is huge in the French tradition. When you study law in a country in the French tradition, there is a good chance the curriculum will contain two mandatory courses on administrative law—one general and one on administrative procedure. I used to think that the enormous attention to administrative law was "normal", given the size of the public sector. Yet when I learned more about other legal systems I noticed that administrative law was thinner in Germany and the Netherlands, and much thinner in the U.S.

For instance, my appointment as a professor in Utrecht (the Netherlands) was governed by contract law, while my appointment as a professor in Ghent (Belgium) fell under administrative law. There are also several famous Dutch and German contract cases dealing with public procurement (like *Plas v. Valburg*, Hoge Read 18 June 1982, *NJ* 1983, 723 (the Netherlands)). In France and Belgium such cases would end up in administrative law books, but in the Netherlands and Germany, they end up in contract law books. Moreover, there are separate administrative courts in the French tradition (though also in the German tradition), but such courts are largely non-existent in the U.S. (where public authorities can be sued in regular courts). In the U.S., the view is that a public authority is just a party like everybody else.

How can we explain the fact that administrative law is so expansive in the French tradition? Two elements play a role. First, the top of the executive branch does not trust judges. Therefore, they want to be sued in a separate court system, that falls within the executive branch (believe it or not, the *Conseil d'etat*, that is, the French supreme court for administrative law, belongs to the executive branch, not the judicial branch!). Secondly, they do not want to fall under the normal rules of contract, property and tort law (as they would in the U.S.). They want their own exceptional rules instead. They do not want to go so far as Inca law, where the leader stood above the law (they still want to have system with a "rule of law"), but it should be their own rules—not the rules that apply to all citizens more generally.

25. Contract law

If the largest differences between common and civil law exist in procedure, the smallest probably exist in contract law. Still, there are huge terminological and philosophical differences in contract law. At the end of the day, however, the result is usually the same.

False difference: specific performance versus damages. When you open a comparative law book dealing with contracts, you will read that there is a big difference between common and civil law regarding remedies for breach of contract. In the common law, damages are the rule and specific performance is the exception. In the civil law, specific performance is the rule and damages are the exception. In reality, the differences are small or non-existent because different definitions of specific performance and damages are used.

Suppose I promise to build a house for you but I don't keep my promise. Can you apply specific performance, forcing me to build a house for you under a threat of a criminal sanction? Or is it fine if I just pay you damages based on your loss? What all modern legal systems do now is none of these but a third alternative: substitute performance by a third party. Another builder will be asked to complete the building, and if that other builder is more expensive than I was, I pay the difference.

Substitute performance is considered specific performance in France because the promisee (i.e., the victim of the breach) receives 100% of the house she wanted. It is considered damages in the U.S. because eventually I don't have to perform specifically as promised but I only pay monetary compensation. More specifically it is called "market damages" in the U.S. In Germany, §887 of the Procedural Code (the *Zivilprozessordnung*, ZPO) states that specific performance cannot be asked if a third party can deliver the service. So, substitute performance is framed as a procedural exception on specific performance.

In well-developed markets like France, Germany or the U.S., substitute performance is the remedy applied in 95% of the cases. Indeed, it is rare that only one company in the country can deliver a certain product or service. Yet because of these terminological differences, French lawyers keep telling themselves that specific performance is the normal remedy in their country. And Americans keep telling themselves that damages is the normal remedy, as exemplified in Holmes' famous quote (*The common law*, 1881, 301):

> the only universal consequence of a legally binding promise is that the law makes the promisor pay damages if the promised act does not come to pass.

False difference: penalty clauses. If you open a comparative law book, you will read that under civil law, penalty clauses are allowed. Under Anglo-American law, penalty clauses are prohibited. You will also read that penalty clauses induce specific performance, so that the positive attitude of civil law countries is no surprise. Is this correct? Unfortunately, there is terminological confusion at the basis of this belief. To understand this confusion, keep in mind there is a distinction made in American law between penalty clauses, liquidated damages and underliquidated damages. These three all fall under the umbrella of "stipulated damages". They are the compensation for breach that the parties put in their contracts. So, under American terminology "stipulated damages" is the general term that can refer to either penalty clauses, liquidated damages and underliquidated damages.

Penalty clauses are deliberately set above the "real losses", i.e., the losses as defined by the expectation measure. Liquidated damages are deliberately set at a level that corresponds to the expectation measure. Underliquidated damages are deliberately set below the expectation measure (for instance to reflect the reliance measure or the restitution measure).

The American penalty doctrine states that penalty clauses (which are intended to be supra-compensatory) are forbidden, while liquidated damages and underliquidated damages are allowed. In other words, overcompensation is forbidden but correct compensation and undercompensation is allowed.

This penalty doctrine makes economic sense. Penalty clauses are not such a great idea, because they lead to overperformance (i.e., they make the promisor perform even if the costs have become so high that the performance is no longer desirable), they are a form of overinsurance (overpaying the promisee for the losses she incurred), and they give the promisee an incentive to try to make the promisor breach.

Now back to France. Article 1226 of the Napoleonic code defines "clause penal" as stipulated damages, not as a penalty clause:

- Article 1226 C.C.: "A penal clause ("clause penal") is a clause whereby a person promises to pay a fixed sum by way of damages in the event he would fail to perform the contract."
- Article 1152 C.C. first sentence (*original art. in 1804*): "When the agreement provides that a party who fails to perform it shall pay a certain sum by way of damages, no larger or smaller sum may be awarded to the other party."
- Article 1152 C.C. second and third sentence (*added in 1975*): "Nonetheless, the judge may, of his own motion, moderate or increase the penalty which was agreed if it is manifestly excessive or derisory. Any provision to the contrary shall be of no effect."

Article 1152 C.C. first sentence states that stipulated damages are in principle valid, but the second and third sentence, which were later added to codify a practice of the courts, state that penalty clauses and underliquidated damages may be decreased or increased, respectively. To be fair, the text does not literally say that courts have to do this—only that they are allowed to do this, so there is some uncertainty surrounding the outcome.

Similarly, §343 of the German civil code states the following:

- §343 BGB: "(1) If a forfeited penalty is disproportionately high, it may be reduced to a reasonable amount by judicial decree on the application of the debtor…"

§348 of the commercial code states that:

- §348 HGB: "A contract penalty, promised by a merchant operating a commercial concern, cannot be reduced on the basis of the provisions of §343 BGB."

But courts reduce penalty clauses promised by a merchant (falling under §348 HGB) on the basis of §242 BGB. So, in Germany, the enforcement of penalty clauses is considered to be contrary to good faith.

Objective versus subjective theory. A century ago, there was a big differ-ence between common and civil law regarding the formation of contracts. In common law countries, the objective theory was applied, while in civil law the subjective theory was applied.

Under the objective theory, it is irrelevant what you were thinking. If your outside behavior suggested that you agreed to the contract, you are bound.

The poster child of the objective theory is *Lucy v. Zehmer.* Zehmer acted as if he wanted to sell his farm, just as a practical joke to fool Lucy. Lucy thought it was for real. The court decided that there was a contract, because a reasonable person in the situation of Lucy would also have thought Zehmer was serious. In *Leonard v. Pepsico,* on the other hand, Pepsico had made an advertisement in which it jokingly stated that for 7,000,000 Pepsi points a military airplane could be earned. Pepsico won, because the court decided that a reasonable person in Leonard's place would have known it was a joke.

The subjective theory, however, tries to determine what people were really thinking. A contract requires a true meeting of minds. So, joke maker Zehmer would have won the case in France.

At a philosophical level, there is a connection between pragmatism, which is popular in the U.S., and the objective theory. In terms of psychology, there is a connection between the objective theory and behavioralism, which is also popular in the U.S. On the other hand, there is a connection between the subjective theory and Freudian depth psychology, both of which are popular on the European continent.

Differences have become smaller though, in that civil law countries have developed reliance doctrines to give an incentive to communicate more carefully.

Unilateral mistake. This is big in civil law countries because of the sub-jective theory. Since a true meeting of minds is required for a contract, a mistake by one of the parties is enough to prevent a contract from being formed. The idea is that consent is no true consent if it was based on a unilateral mistake.

Consider the *Poussin* case in France (Court of Cassation 13 December 1983). A family thought they owned a real Poussin but before selling it they asked advice of an expert. The expert mistakenly thought it was *not* a Poussin. So the family sold it for little money, and it quickly ended up in the world-famous museum the Louvre in Paris. The family got their painting back because the court judged that the owner had not given true consent, but only consent based on unilateral mistake.

The Napoleonic civil code was extreme in protecting the mistaken party:

- Article 1109 Civil Code: "There is no valid consent if the consent was only given as the result of error . . . "
- Art. 1110 Civil Code: "Error is a cause of nullity of an agreement only when it goes to the *very substance* of the object of the agreement. It is not a ground of nullity when it relates only to the person with whom a party intends a contract, unless the consideration of that person was the principal purpose of the agreement." [Italics added]

To prevent unilateral mistake from being used too often as a cheap excuse to get out of a contract, French courts developed a rule that the mistake must be excusable. In the *Poussin* case, though, the mistake was considered excusable because non-experts placed in the same position would also have relied on the expert's mistaken report.

In the U.S., it is nearly fair to say that unilateral mistake does not exist. This has to do with the Protestant culture of taking responsibility. If I make a mistake, and nobody is to blame, I should take responsibility for my own mistake. If the other party made me make a mistake by telling lies, then I can get out of the contract, not on the basis of mistake but on the basis of misrepresentation. If both parties made the mistake, then we are talking about a risk issue, dealt with under the doctrine of *mutual* mistake.

The doctrine of mutual mistake is big in the U.S. The question is how the parties allocated the risk. In *Wood v. Boyton* (1885), a farmer had discovered a stone and sold it for $1 to a jeweler, and neither of them knew what it was. Later it turned out to be a diamond, sold by the jeweler for $600. When the farmer heard about this, he went to court, trying to get the diamond back, but the court concluded that the parties had allocated the risk of the stone being more or less worth to the jeweler.

The only cases in which American courts apply the doctrine of *unilateral* mistake is when contractors or subcontractors make a mistake in preparing a bid but then realize they made a mistake before the job started and before the other party started to rely on the bid. Upon closer inspection, it would be more precise to see this as an application of a lesion doctrine. American courts, however, don't have a lesion doctrine, so they use the unilateral mistake doctrine to obtain a fair outcome.

The duty to disclose is big in the U.S. In contract law, there is a duty to reveal latent effects. If you know your house has termite damage, you have to spontaneously reveal that. To be fair, a similar duty to disclose exists in France and Germany. U.S. law goes way beyond that though. Stock-listed corporations have far-reaching disclosure duties under the SEC regulations. For instance, pursuant to section 12 of the Securities Exchange Act of 1934, stock-listed corporations are required to file a registration statement; the corporations are also obligated to file annual reports, quarterly reports and current reports. Late filing may cause severe consequence, such as deregistering the securities by the authority. One step further, the Sarbanes-Oxley Act requires the stock-listed corporations to submit earlier and more complete information that directly or indirectly influences investors' financial decisions.

The first time a visitor goes to an American doctor, she may be shocked to see all the paperwork that needs to be filled out and signed. For instance, doctors must disclose their privacy policies and need written proof that the patient has received a copy of the privacy policy.

In product liability, there is a far-reaching duty to warn that may preempt the duty to take care. Consider the *McDonald's* case. In February 1992, 79-year-old Stella Liebeck ordered coffee at the drive-thru of a local McDonald's restaurant. She placed the coffee cup between her knees and attempted to remove the lid, but she spilled the coffee on her lap. Liebeck was taken to the hospital, where doctors determined that she had suffered third-degree burns over 6% of her skin. Her burns required skin grafts and a seven-day hospital stay. Two years of treatment followed. She attempted to settle with McDonald's for $20,000 to cover medical costs, but McDonald's offered only $800. Liebeck filed suit after McDonald's refused to increase their settlement offer. McDonald's required its franchises to serve coffee at a temperature between 180–190 degrees Fahrenheit (83–88 degrees Celsius). They also knew that their coffee was served at least 20 to 50 degrees higher temperature than at other restaurants. From 1982 to 1992, McDonald's settled more than 700 incidents of scalding coffee burns.

The jury found that McDonald's had breached its implied warranty of merchantability and implied warranty of fitness for particular purpose and also engaged in wilful, reckless, malicious, or wanton conduct. Liebeck was awarded $2.7 million in punitive damages, later reduced by the judge to $480,000; in addition, Liebeck was awarded $640,000 in compensatory damages. McDonald's eventually settled the case for an undisclosed amount.

Did McDonald's lower the temperature after this incident? No, it didn't. It printed a warning on its coffee. Starbucks later followed. It prints on its cups, "Careful, the beverage you're about to enjoy is extremely hot."

Why is the duty to disclose so big in the U.S.? One reason is that the culture has an extraordinarily strong aversion for dishonesty. The culture also puts much emphasis on individual responsibility of independent decision makers, but that requires individuals to have sufficient information. Another reason is political.[1] Washington, D.C., is often at a gridlock when the majority in the House of Representatives, the majority in the Senate, and the President do not belong to the same party. Disclosure is something all parties can agree on. The Republicans like it because it is not the type of invasive regulation that businesses dislike. The Democrats like it because it is some form of intervention and some form is better than no intervention at all.

Lesion doctrine only in civil law countries. In late Roman law, there was a rule (*laesio enormis*) that stated that if land was sold for less than half of the normal price, the sale could be annulled. Medieval lawyers generalized this rule to all goods, creating a just price doctrine. Remainders of this lesion doctrine still exist in civil law countries. Article 1674 of the Napoleonic Civil Code gave the seller of land two years to avoid the sale if the price was less than seven-twelfths of the current value of the land. A similar rule exists in Louisiana.

---

[1]   Ben-Shahar and Schneider, *More Than You Want to Know: The Failure of Mandated Disclosure* (Princeton University Press, 2014).

While there is no general lesion doctrine in the U.S., there are some courts that apply the unconscionability doctrine to excessive prices paid by consumers, and courts that use the unilateral mistake doctrine to bail out contractors who made an unrealistically low bid.

The consideration requirement. According to standard doctrine in the U.S., contracts need to have consideration to be binding. Consideration is defined as what has been bargained for. Each party needs consideration. Therefore, each party needs to get something out of the deal. That something can be a material good, an immaterial good like a patent license, or a service, but it cannot be the altruistic pleasure received from a gift. Consideration can be seen as a legal motive. Each party needs a motive, but the motive needs to be something concrete that was bargained for.

Nearly all types of contract have consideration. If I buy a pound of tomatoes for $1.99, then getting the tomatoes is consideration for me to give up my $1.99 and getting my $1.99 is the merchant's consideration to give up the tomatoes. If I remodel your basement for you for $100,000, the value of my work is your consideration and the $100,000 is my consideration.

When is there no consideration for gift promises and similar one-sided transactions? If your uncle promises to give you $5,000 on your 21st birthday, and there are no strings attached, then this gift promise is not legally binding. If there are strings attached, for instance that you have to quit smoking, drinking, and gambling until your 21st birthday, then there is consideration, because your uncle got something out of the deal.

Does this mean that all gifts you received from your grandmother for New Year can be claimed back? No, that is not an outcome the consideration doctrine wants to obtain. Technically, this is achieved by the element of the doctrine that says that consideration makes the promise unenforceable but not invalid. A given gift does not have to be enforced anymore because it has already been performed. Therefore, given gifts remain with the recipient.

The common law has carved out other exceptions. If there are no strings attached, but you start to rely on the fact that you expect to receive money in the future, then the gift promise is enforceable. In *Ricketts v. Scothorn* (1898), a grandfather promised to pay his granddaughter $2,000 as soon as he had some cash available, and expressed the hope that she would quit her job. She quit her job but her grandfather died before he gave her the money. The court made the promise enforceable, not because there was consideration (there wasn't since there was only a desire and no strict conditions attached) but because there was "promissory estoppel".

Do other countries have the consideration requirement as well? Well, they used to have such a thing as the "cause" requirement, which is very similar. But in the German civil code (BGB) of 1900, causa was dropped because it was seen as an overly technical complication. In 2016, even France dropped the causa requirement.

Are all gift promises now enforceable in France? No. At its core, the consideration doctrine is gift regulation, and France has some specific rules on gifts. Gift promises are only binding in France if the donor went to a notary to record the gift promise. A notary is quite different in France than in the U.S. In France, it is a trained lawyer (with a law degree). French notaries read aloud the act they have drafted, so the procedure serves as a little ceremony. This, in turn, stops impulsive decisions to make gifts in the future.

Trusts in the U.S. Is there no way in the U.S. to make a pure gift promise enforceable? Yes there is—through a trust. A trust is something unique in the common law. Although it could be compared to a non-profit institution with legal personality, its goal can be anything, including "Give $5,000 to my nephew on his 21st birthday irrespective of whether he drank, smoked or gambled." A trust can also be made irrevocable, making it impossible to later go back on the promise and take back the $5,000. How does a trust get around the requirement of consideration? By paying now. Remember, a gift promise is not enforceable, but a given gift (to a trust) cannot be taken back. So, uncles who want to make binding gift promises can go to a notary in France or set up a trust in the U.S. The result is that only well-conceived gift promises are enforceable. The legal system protects gift promisors against their own impulsivity, in different ways.

Revocability of offers. A contract requires mutual assent in all legal systems. As a matter of fact, mutual assent is what distinguishes a contract from a tort (where no party gave assent) or unjust enrichment (where sometimes one but never two parties gave assent).

The first to approve a proposal is called the offeror. When you are the second to approve, you are the one who accepted. Offer and acceptance differ only with respect to the timing. The first to say yes is the offeror, the second to say yes is the offeree. That is the case in all legal systems.

What differs is whether an offer can be revoked. Suppose I make you a proposal to remodel your kitchen for $100,000, and one hour later, while you are still thinking about it, I revoke my offer without telling you the reason. Can I revoke the offer? Not in Germany, where offers are irrevocable unless the offeror stated clearly that the offer was revocable. I can revoke the offer in France, where the rule is that all offers are revocable unless I made it clear that they are irrevocable. In England, it is the extreme opposite—I can't even make an offer irrevocable. The reason is that there is no consideration at the side of the offeror. I made a promise (to keep the offer open for a certain time) but you didn't do something in return. At most, there may be some cases in which promissory estoppel is accepted—when you started to make expenses to examine the offer, relying on the fact I promised to keep the offer open.

How about in the U.S.? Here, the normal rule is that offers are revocable but if I make it clear that my offer is revocable, I can make a *firm offer* that is binding in many states, and that is binding under §2-205 UCC if the offer is made in writing and is made by the merchant.

A related question is whether an advertisement should be seen as an offer. The merchant behind the advertisement is the first to accept the deal, so that's the offeror, isn't it? Not so in England and the U.S. Consumers naturally want to consider it an offer, but the merchant naturally prefers not to be bound, just in case the advertisement is such a success that the merchant runs out of stock and is still left with obligations to customers. In Germany, advertisements are offers until stock is exhausted. Also in France, they are conditional offers (that is, until stock is exhausted). In England and the U.S., they are no more than invitations to make offers, unless the advertisement says differently, or the quantity is fixed (e.g., "First come first serve"). So, if you go to Walmart, lay the $1.99 tomatoes in your cart and present them to the cashier, you make the offer, and if Walmart accepts your payment, it accepts your offer and there is a contract. (So, in the U.S., you can go shopping, come home, and tell your family, "I made Walmart many offers and they accepted them all.")

How about goods displayed in windows with price tags, or in shops with prices indicated? In France, these are offers, so if I put them into my cart and lay them on the cashier's desk, the shop is bound. If the price was a mistake, the shop is still bound, unless the mistake was so gigantic that I should have known it was a mistake. In Germany, England, and the U.S., such displayed goods are no more than an invitation to make an offer. The consumer makes the offer by going to the cashier and the shop accepts by accepting the consumer's money. So, when the posted price was a mistake, the shop can still get out of the deal.

In short, American and English law is more concerned with helping businesses, while French law is most concerned with helping consumers.

Precontractual liability and the duty of good faith. In the U.S., it is seen as a general principle that contracts must be performed in good faith. Civil law countries take it one step further and say that even before a contract is formed, negotiations need to be done in good faith. English law, at the other extreme of the spectrum, does not have a doctrine of good faith. In England, you have to follow all the detailed rules about contract law, but there is no general duty of good faith on top of those rules.

The doctrine of good faith was developed in medieval times, by lawyers who were often also theologians. In Christian (and Jewish and Muslim) religion, it is not only important to follow the rules but it should be done with a good heart, with the best of intentions. This is what good faith is at its core. Why is there no faith duty in English law? Because English law was developed separately, with little European influence, just case by case, detailed rule by detailed rule at English courts. Why is there, then, a good faith rule in the U.S.? Because of all the German immigrants, many of whom became law professors! But why not in the precontractual stage? Because that is a more recent, 20th century evolution in German law.

Does this mean, in the U.S., that precontractual bad faith behavior goes unpunished? No. Some American courts extend the misrepresentation doctrine to also include cases where a misrepresentation was made and no contract was formed. That was the case in *Markov v. ABC Transfer & Storage Co.* (1969). The lessor of warehouse facilities suggested to the lessee that it intended to renew the lease; the lessor did not intend to renew the lease but wanted to have the premises occupied during the negotiations for their sale. The court decided there was misrepresentation.

26. Property law and inheritance law

Touch and concern (instead of prohibition of positive servitudes). In feudal times, the relationship between a farmer and the local lord was contractual. The contract stipulated not only that the farmer had to pay a part of his harvest, but also that the farmer had to do specific services. For instance, when the lord gave a party, the farmer had to serve food to the guests. That probably made sense at that time. There wasn't a developed catering market, not even a developed labor market, and the farmer couldn't work on the field anyway during winter or at night.

The French Revolution wanted to break with feudal traditions. The Napoleonic Code (1804) forbade positive easements, that is, easements where the owner of the land had to do something, rather than tolerate something. In England, there was never such a radical reaction against feudalism. Does this mean that, if you own property, you can be called on to help serve food on a nearby mansion? No. Anglo-American tort law has a "touch and concern" requirement for easements. Serving at a party has nothing to do with the land itself. There is no touch or concern. So the owner of that land doesn't have to do it.

Adverse possession and the weak protection of the good faith purchaser. Adverse possession means that the goods are in the hands ("possessed') of someone who believes she's the owner but in reality she is not the owner. How can this happen? Maybe she bought the land from someone who thought he inherited the land but was disinherited through a will that was later found. Maybe she bought a moveable object, like a painting, not knowing it was stolen.

The law here must balance two things. First, it does not want to help thieves and negligent people. It can achieve this result by giving the true owner the right to claim the goods back at any time. This depresses the market price for potentially stolen goods. At the same time, it wants to give an incentive to people who buy a painting to check whether the painting is potentially stolen. Secondly, it wants to create legal certainty in the market. This is achieved by giving good faith adverse possessors full protection. If you bought the painting, you can keep it. You can be sure.

As it turns out, the U.S. is at one extreme, giving extreme protection to the original owner. Italy is at the other extreme, giving quasi full protection to adverse possessors. How to explain this difference? The universalist ethics might play a role here. In the U.S., the truth must come out and the good must return to the true owner. In Italy, there is the catholic culture of forgiving and moving on.

The German land register system. In Germany, whoever's name is written in the land register is the official owner. If two different people claim to be the true owner, the outcome is that the one whose name is in the land register wins the case. Therefore, if someone else sells my home, thinking she is the true owner of my house, does that mean that I have to leave my home? To prevent this, writing a new name in the land register requires a mini procedure in Germany, where a judge will invite me, the current owner, to appear in front of her. In the U.S., the system does not need a prior procedure every time there is a transfer, but I need to buy "title insurance" just in case someone else will show up who turns out to be the true owner.

No allemansrett in the United States. Allemansrett is a Scandinavian word. It means that all men (and women) have a right to walk in forests, even privately owned ones. If you go to the European Alps, you can walk in any forest and climb any mountain that you see. What is the point of owning a wooded area if anyone on this planet can walk in it? Well, the owner still has the hunting rights, grazing rights, and timber rights.

Thus, when I moved with my family to the U.S., we were in for a rude awakening. We drove southwest of St. Louis to go climb one of the highest hills. When we had hiked 15 minutes, we were stopped by someone who turned out to be the true owner of the entire hill. He said we were trespassing on private property and that we had to leave immediately.

To be fair, the U.S. has many state parks. But in the U.S., land is either public or private. In Europe, land can be in between, that is, privately owned but with a public easement so that "all men" can walk there.

Why is there then "*allemansrett*" in Austria, to name but one country? Well, a few centuries ago there was private property without *allemansrett*. The forests were owned by a small group of wealthy families. But then the rule was changed.

No public easements for skiing in the U.S. In the U.S., skiing is underdeveloped. The number of Americans who ski is small compared to the number of Europeans who ski. In the U.S., skiing is for the relatively wealthy—say, the top 10%. In Europe, skiing is also for the middle class— say, the top 50%.

To be fair, the American ski regions are further away from the regions with dense populations. But the real reason is that skiing is more expensive in the U.S. because there is simply less infrastructure. Why?

If you want to start a new ski region in the U.S., you basically have to buy a whole mountain. You are then the private owner of the mountain and only let in people who buy a ski pass. In Europe, you can simply connect fields of farmers. The farmers will receive some compensation but they cannot veto certain ski slopes. Moreover, farmers have to put down their wires when winter starts.

Taking under eminent domain. In which country is it harder to take land under eminent domain: the U.S., France, or China? You probably think it is the U.S. because the U.S. is the country with the strongest ideological emphasis on private property. In reality, it is easier to take land under eminent domain in the U.S. than in France or China. In all countries, a taking is only possible if it is in the general interest, but in the U.S., since the *Kelo* case, the general interest is whatever the city defines as general interest. So, if my own university, Washington University, needs to expand, it can do so under eminent domain as long as the city of St. Louis agrees. If Walmart needs a whole block for a new store, it only needs to find a city that needs local tax income and it can flatten a whole block in the general interest.

Forced heirship. In the U.S., there is no such thing as forced heirship. People can leave their inheritance to whoever they want. They don't have to leave anything to their children.

This stands in stark contrast with the civil law tradition of forced heirship—a tradition that goes back to Roman law. The Code Napoleon has far-reaching restrictions for the benefit of the children. If a parent has one child, at least 50% must go to that child. If there are two children, then at least 66% goes to them. If there are three or more children, at least 75% goes to them. In that case, the parent can freely decide on only 25% of the assets.

27. Intellectual property law

Moral rights. In 1991, two young Belgians were on their way to having an international hit record with a techno version of Carl Orff's *Carmina Burana* when the heirs of Carl Orff prevented them from selling further records. The heirs disliked the techno version and thought that it did no justice to what Orff had originally conceived.

In the French copyright tradition (taken over by most European countries), authors have a right to determine what versions of their work are made. Authors have a certain vision of how the work should be performed and can prevent people from performing the work in a way they don't like. Even if artists sell the copyrights, they always keep the moral rights. The French view depicts the artist as a genius, who knows best how his work needs to be performed. (Overall, the law in Europe is primarily meant to protect the individual artist. In the U.S., the art industries, including Hollywood, are protected.)

Moral rights consist of four components. First, the right of integrity, which allows an artist to prevent alterations to her work. Secondly, the right of attribution, which means that the work can only be shown if the artist's name is put on it. In other words, the user of the artistic work must know who is the artist that has made the piece of art. Thirdly, there is the right of disclosure, which gives the artist the right not to have the work exposed to the public as long as it is not ready. Finally, there is the right of retraction, which gives the artist the right to withdraw her work even after she has sold it.

Most civil law countries not only recognize these moral rights but make them even more inalienable. Common law countries including the U.S., on the other hand, do the opposite. They effectively make it unenforceable to stipulate that the artist keeps such rights after she has transferred the other elements of ownership. Amazingly, moral rights that are mandatory in European civil law countries are forbidden in the U.S.

That being said, 11 American states now explicitly recognize moral rights to some extent, and in 1989 Congress approved the federal Visual Artists Rights Act (VARA), which creates moral rights, though only for visual artists.

Droit de suite. Suppose you are an artist and you sell a painting for $10,000. Many years later, the painting is resold for $10 million. Do you get a piece of that amount? Not in most U.S. states, but in California you do. The California Resale Royalty Act (Civil Code, section 986) entitles artists to a share of the sales price when their works are resold (a resale royalty payment). There is a similar rule in the European Union. The goal of this rule is to let the artists participate in the economic success of their work.

Statutory damages in copyright law. In 2008, a few individuals were sued by a few record labels for copyright infringement for file sharing on peer-to-peer (P2P) networks (Depoorter, 2019). One individual was ordered to pay $222,000 in statutory damages for sharing 24 songs online.

Statutory damages are damages written in the statute. They make it unnecessary for the copyright holder to prove the harm.

Statutory damages have a minimum of $750 and a maximum of $150,000. The latter explains why in another case $75 trillion was asked from the operator of a file-sharing network—more than the GDP of the entire world. The court deemed the amount ridiculous, but it nonetheless shows how much stress statutory damages can create, especially since there is always some uncertainty as to whether the court will apply the minimum or the maximum (Depoorter, 2019).

Fair use is broader in the U.S. Fair use means that no permission is needed to use a copyrighted text. For instance, if you want to quote a short passage from this book, you can do so without asking my permission.

Fair use is much broader in the U.S. than in Europe. Suppose you want to broadcast the head-butt Zinedine Zidane gave to an Italian player in the FIFA World Cup in 2006. The video is only a few seconds long. In the U.S., you can do this without asking permission as it is "fair use". In Europe, you have to ask permission, even for a video of a few seconds. A Belgian TV maker recently explained that the fee is so high that they can no longer use short video pieces in TV programs.

28. Tort law and environmental regulation

Punitive damages. Punitive damages are compensation the victim receives in excess of the true losses. For instance, in one of the cases surrounding Merck's drug Vioxx, a Texas jury awarded $7 million compensatory and $25 million punitive damages for a 71-year-old smoking heart patient, who had a fatal heart attack three weeks after taking the product during one week. Here, the multiplier was 25/7 or about factor 3.5. (Ben-Shahar, 2006).

Punitive damages have two functions. First, they may correctly "price" the real loss in cases where many offenses are not successfully sued because of a lack of evidence. Suppose a car driver causes a crash and the loss equals $10,000. The car driver leaves the scene of the accident in an attempt to escape responsibility. Suppose the chance that the driver will be "caught" is 25%. In this case, adding $30,000 punitive damages brings the bill up to $40,000 so that the driver statistically again pays $10,000 (i.e., 25% to pay $40,000 in total).

Secondly, punitive damages may hit hard so that the undesirable behavior will not occur anymore in the future. The goal of punitive damages, then, is not to price but to deter. This was the case in the *Exxon Valdez* case (United States Court of Appeals, Ninth Circuit, 270 F.3d 1215, 7 November 2001, Decided, Kleinfeld, Circuit Judge). In 1989, the oil tanker Exxon Valdez ran aground on a reef in Alaska. The ship spilled 11 million gallons of oil—it was the largest oil accident in U.S. history. As it turned out, the captain of the ship was drunk while in command of the tanker. He had passed command to an over-tired third mate with vague instructions on how to perform a critical maneuver. He had also chosen a course making it more difficult to avoid Bligh Reef. Also, he had made the tanker more difficult to maneuver by placing it on autopilot. As it turned out, Exxon knew of the captain's alcohol relapse after treatment and of the captain's drinking immediately before performing his duties.

The jury awarded $287 million in compensatory damages and $5 billion in punitive damages against Exxon—at that time, the largest punitive damage award in American history. Compared to the original $287 million, the punitive damages were factor 17. Eventually the U.S. Supreme Court further reduced punitive damages on 25 June 2008 to an amount equal to the compensatory damages (which were at that time calculated as $507.5 million).

Punitive damages exist in the U.S. but can rarely be used in England and not in civil law countries. How do these countries *make up* with a lower probability of detection, and how do they deter undesirable acts? They add a fine to the bill. For instance, the car driver may pay $10,000 in tort damages (which goes to the victim) and $30,000 in criminal fines (which goes to the government). Why do civil law countries prefer fines and prosecutors to do the job? Because they have a top-down system that puts more trust in a prosecutor and less in individual parties.

No cumulation of tort, contract, and unjust enrichment. In the state of Missouri, there lives a reptile that looks like a snake because it has no legs but it also has some characteristic of a lizard because it can, for instance, blink its eyes. Is this a snake or a lizard or both? Scientists decided that it had to be one of these two, and they decided it is a special lizard.

In France, there is a strict non-cumulation rule when it comes to contract law, tort law, consumer law and unjust enrichment. The plaintiff has to choose one and claim that one. Indeed, in the civil law there is the scientific idea that all rules need to be well-ordered. This is a more general scientific idea. An animal is either a lizard or a snake, but it can't be both.

American law is very different. Attorneys typically will sue on the basis of all possible fields. In a contracts case, they will claim that the undesirable behavior was also a tort, or that the money should be paid also to prevent unjust enrichment. In addition, they will try to claim the act violated consumer protection statutes, which are usually more generous to plaintiffs than simple contract law. It is like throwing many pies to the wall and hoping that at least one will stick.

Why is American law different? One reason is its inductive reasoning, based on an analogy with cases. Typically, a case has many dimensions and, therefore, more analogies to other cases than just one. The second reason is simply the lack of interest in the structure of the law. The mentality is one of, "don't change what works, and whatever set of rules works is fine".

Are common law countries safer? Michael Smith (2005) analysed the evolution of motor vehicle and other accident fatalities over 50 years (1950–2000) and he concluded that the common law Scandinavian and German fatalities do not differ significantly. They are lower than countries of the French family, which in turn are lower than the socialist family. A remarkable fact is that the German family originally had the highest of all fatalities, but over time it evolved to fatality rates comparable with common law countries. This suggests that a well-engineered civil law system that relies heavily on safety regulation (like those of the German and Scandinavian family) can be as effective as a common law system that relies on tort law.

However, Smith found a different outcome for other (non-motor vehicle) accident fatalities: here the common law rates were lower than those in the French, Scandinavian and German family. The disparity grew over time. Civil law countries of the German and Scandinavian tradition are probably not as effective here because these accidents are too diverse to be effectively regulated through safety regulation.

More generally, common law countries take tort law more seriously. This probably has a positive effect on the number of accidents.

Environmental policy.[1] The differences between the U.S. and Europe have become smaller in recent decades. The U.S. started much earlier than Europe with the use of emission trading. As a matter of fact, an emission trading system for sulphur dioxide emerged in the 1980s. In Europe, emission trading was introduced only 20 years later when Europe had to implement the Kyoto Protocol. However, as far as the other market-based instrument, corrective taxation, is concerned, the story is the reverse: there are some experiments with the use of tax charges in Europe. In the

---

[1]   See, Faure and Vig.

U.S., interest groups have been much more successful in blocking the introduction of charges.

The largest difference may be regarding enforcement. Environmental liability exists only on paper in Europe—governments rarely enforce environmental policy. Europe came with an Environmental Liability Directive in 2004, but the reports concerning its implementation show that it barely plays a role. The story is different in the U.S. where since CERCLA and the creation of SUPERFUND, liability rules do play an important role, not only for compensation, but also for deterrence. In the U.S., prosecutors go for harsh prosecution based on deterrence; business leaders end up in prison for pollution. In short, European enforcement authorities follow more the compliance-based cooperation strategy whereas in the U.S. a deterrence-based strategy is followed.

29. Corporate law

In the late 1990s, four economists (La Porta, Lopez-de-Silanes, Shleifer, and Vishny) were the first to use large datasets and advanced statistics to determine which country had the best law. They found that common law countries have better, more developed financial markets than civil law countries. They attributed this to the fact that minority shareholders are better protected under the common law. In other words: self-dealing is harder to do in common law countries than in civil law countries, and this is what makes the capital markets thrive.

In one of their follow-up papers (Johnson, La Porta, Lopez-de-Silanes and Shleifer, 2000), the authors explain how "tunneling" is easier in civil law countries. Tunneling is the transfer of resources out of one company to another company (as in removing assets through an underground tunnel.) Tunneling is a form of self-dealing, where profits of one company become profits of another company. Both common law and civil law countries try to prevent self-dealing, but the technique used is different. Common law countries work with the vague standard of "fiduciary duty". It is against the fiduciary duty to virtually steal from minority shareholders. Civil law countries work with a statutory list of practices that are forbidden. They prefer the legal certainty of those lists, and don't like giving so much discretion to courts as common law countries do.

The problem is that, when 20 forms of self-dealing are listed in those statutes, but self-dealing form number 21 is invented, this is allowed in civil law countries. The court has to say, "What you did is unfair but it is legal." In common law countries, number 21 can be attacked in court on the basis of the vague fiduciary duty towards the first company.

In corporations, leaders (like directors or CEOs) work with money that is largely belonging to other people. Corporate law is a set of rules that prevents self-dealing in all its forms. When corporate law is underdeveloped, self-dealing may take place on a massive scale. This is what happened during the rapid mass privatization of state-owned enterprises in Russia in the 1990s. American transition economists had positively advised on this rapid privatization but had overlooked that in Western market economies private corporations operate within a strict legal framework (corporate law and securities regulation), the purpose of which is to prevent self-dealing. Russia lacked such a legal framework, and its mass privatization resulted in mass self-dealing.

What other differences exist in corporate law? Hansmann and Kraakman (2001) argue that the deeper tendency in the corporate law system is toward convergence. The idea that the fundamental goal of corporate law is the maximization of long-term shareholder value seems now to be generally accepted. Still, on paper, the goal of German corporate law is not shareholder value maximization but stakeholder interest maximization. Employees are allowed to elect half of the members of the board of directors in all large German firms.

30. Bankruptcy law

Old law was harsh for insolvent debtors. Debts were never forgiven. In many cases, debtors were pushed into slavery. In other cases, debtors risked criminal sanctions—even the death penalty.

Harsh punishment makes sense when bankrupt debtors fraudulently misrepresent the risk, or when they move assets to friends or family on the eve of bankruptcy. However, when insolvency is a matter of bad luck, harsh sanctions discourage risk-taking and entrepreneurship. In that case, the only way to avoid those sanctions is: don't set up a business. Old law was unable to distinguish the two. Therefore, it treated all debtors alike, punishing them all harshly. As the capacity of legal systems increased, bankruptcy became softer, offering a fresh start to unlucky debtors, and jail to fraudulent debtors.

The U.S. has taken the lead in the move from harsh to soft sanctions. The modern idea is that bankruptcy is like an accident: you deserve a fresh start. If the business is sound in itself, its assets will not even be liquidated, but Chapter 11 of the Bankruptcy Code will be applied, offering a reorganization supervised by the court. Most western countries followed this trend by reforming their bankruptcy code in the 1980s onwards. Still, many civil law countries are not as far advanced as the U.S.—for instance, they may not have personal bankruptcy provisions.

31. Labor and employment law

Labor law in the U.S. Americans make a distinction between labor law and employment law. Labor law is the law related to collective negotiations. Employment law refers to the law of the employment relationship apart from collective bargaining. In Europe, the term "labor law" is used in a broader definition, and includes individual labor contracts (which include all types of employment contracts) as well as collective labor law (unions, collective agreements ...). In the U.S., the term labor law has a narrower definition; there the term is only used to refer to the law of collective bargaining.

In the U.S. union membership as a proportion of total employment has declined over the past few decades. Only a small fraction of the economy falls under labor law now—less than 10% of the employees in the private sector is a member of a union.[1] That fraction is much higher in most European countries.

Employment at will versus just cause. One of the most striking differences between American and European employment law is the American at-will doctrine. According to this doctrine, employment contracts can be terminated at any time and for any reason (a good, a bad, or no reason at all) by either party. Though the at-will doctrine has been eroded over the years, it is still the default rule in many states.

At the other side of the spectrum is the just cause termination. This means that workers can only be fired for a good reason. Under "just cause" dismissal protection, the employee cannot be dismissed unless the employer can prove that he has good reasons for doing so, for instance because the employee did not fulfill his obligations, or because economic

---

[1]   Jake Rosenfeld, *What Unions No Longer Do* (Harvard University Press, 2014) 3.

reasons induce him to reduce the number of employees, etc. This puts the burden of evidence on the employer's shoulders. The most extreme form of protection is tenure, where the employee may not even be dismissed for economic reasons (only for serious misconduct or shirking).

In between is termination at will but with a notice period. Longer notice periods are a simple form of increased protection. Here, the at-will rule remains the starting point of the regime, but the notice period reduced the chance of temporary unemployment between two jobs.

All these regimes can be observed in American as well as in European employment markets. There is a general tendency, however, for European employment relationships to be governed by stronger protection regimes. How can we explain this?

First, the U.S. has a larger market, so it is easier to find a similar job. Population wise, the European Union forms an even larger labor market, but language barriers and a stay-where-you-are-born culture make real markets even smaller than the size of the individual member state of the EU. Thus when there is a conflict the three fundamental options are loyalty (saying nothing), voice (trying to change from the inside out), and exit (leaving the company). The U.S. is one of the largest labor markets, so exit is relatively a better option than loyalty or voice.

Secondly, there is a culture of freedom and initiative taking in America. Thirdly, there is not a family-based employer culture, but a project-based culture. Americans more easily accept that they lose their job when their employer starts a different project.

The just-cause doctrine is more common in Europe, though it may lose prominence as the European Union gets more successful in effectively establishing a European labor market. However, labor mobility may never get as high as in the U.S. due to language barriers, so American and European employment law may never converge totally.

How about notice-based protection? Here it makes sense that these periods tend to be shorter in the larger labor market of the U.S. than in the smaller, local markets within member states of Europe.

Covenants not to compete. Silicon Valley, a small area south of San Francisco, is the leading geographic success story of recent decades. Why exactly did this happen in North California? One answer is that Silicon Valley is close to Stanford University. But Stanford is not the only university with a strong engineering department. Why didn't these tech companies locate in Massachusetts, close to the leading engineering school MIT?

As it turns out, there is a location near MIT that is full of businesses. It is called Route 128 (in Massachusetts, close to MIT). But it never became such a center of innovation as Silicon Valley.

Here is the hypothesis of Ronald Gilson: the advantage of California is that covenants not to compete are forbidden in that state. In Massachusetts, on the other hand, covenants not to compete are legally binding.

A covenant not to compete is a term in an employment contract that states that, should the employee leave the company, she can't start working for a competing company in the neighborhood. The goal of a "noncompete" is to prevent that businesses free riding on the efforts of the first company. Without a noncompete, a competing company could easily hire away some of the best employees of a company that has already invested substantively in these workers.

In a sense, the employment market in Silicon Valley is like the situation for bikes in Amsterdam in the 1970s. Your bike is stolen but you need a bike; so you in turn steal one. You leave the bike at your point of destination, where it is again stolen and so you steal another bike. At the end of the day, bikes become commons that can work if all participants do the same.

But wait—if noncompetes prevent a form of stealing, why doesn't Massachusetts have an advantage over California? Well, for pharmaceuticals that may very well be the case. But in IT, innovation is incremental. About 99% of an app is existing know-how, and 1% is the difference that brings the innovation. So in IT, "stealing" each other's know-how is good because it prevents all companies needing to reinvent the wheel.

In California noncompetition clauses are unenforceable, in Massachusetts they are allowed. Hence, in California it is easier to "steal" ideas and even know-how from competing IT companies by hiring their workers.

Paradoxically, this produces better results. Gilson attributes this to special characteristics of the IT sector (cumulative technology, where each new innovation differs only marginally from a previous innovation). While the absence of noncompetition clauses allows for some free riding, this disadvantage is outweighed by the more efficient learning and idea exchange processes.

How about other countries? In most, the rule is like in Massachusetts: noncompetes are allowed, if they are reasonable in time (for instance, two years) and geography (for instance, 10 miles). California is an outlier.

32. Antitrust law

An American invention. Antitrust law, or "competition law" as it is called elsewhere on the planet, is an American invention. It started with the Sherman Act in 1890, later followed by the Clayton Act in 1914. European countries followed much later, when the first European international economic organizations were built after World War II. Most other countries developed antitrust law in the 1990s to get good grades from the World Bank or the IMF. Some developing countries still don't have antitrust law.

Mimicking the U.S. Europe has always looked up to American antitrust law. In the U.S., however, there has been a shift from the Harvard School (pro more intervention) to the Chicago School (pro less intervention). Europe has followed the Harvard School rather than the Chicago School. As a result, the European Union is more forbidding.

Abuse of dominant position. That Europe forbids more is clear when it comes to section 2 of the Sherman Act and Article 82 (formerly Article 102) of the EC Treaty. For instance, Europe automatically forbids price discrimination in loyalty programs. The U.S. no longer has a per se rule, but under the rule of reason it is quite lenient:

- Sherman Act, section 2 (15 U.S. Code § 2): "Every person who shall monopolize, or attempt to monopolize, or combine or conspire with any other person or persons, to monopolize any part of the trade or commerce among the several States, or with foreign nations, shall be deemed guilty of a felony, and, on conviction thereof, shall be punished by fine not exceeding $100,000,000 if a corporation, or, if any other person, $1,000,000, or by imprisonment not exceeding 10 years, or by both said punishments, in the discretion of the court."
- Article 82 of the EC Treaty: "Any abuse by one or more undertakings of a dominant position within the common market or in a substantial part of it shall be prohibited as incompatible with the common market insofar as it may affect trade between Member States. Such abuse may, in particular, consist in: (a) directly or indirectly imposing unfair pur-

chase or selling prices or other unfair trading conditions; (b) limiting production, markets or technical development to the prejudice of consumers; (c) applying dissimilar conditions to equivalent transactions with other trading parties, thereby placing them at a competitive disadvantage; (d) making the conclusion of contracts subject to acceptance by the other parties of supplementary obligations which, by their nature or according to commercial usage, have no connection with the subject of such contracts."

Antitrust law is very expensive law. Antitrust enforcement requires complicated fact-finding, including calculating market shares, price elasticities and potential consumer benefits. Cases take weeks or even years and require teams of highly specialized lawyers and economists.

The benefit of more competition may be high, though. Cartels and monopolists distort prices and significantly reduce allocative efficiency. So, the reason why antitrust law was until recently virtually nonexistent is not that the benefits per case are low; the reason is that these cases require an incredible amount of work.

This may explain why competition law was virtually nonexistent before the American Sherman Act in 1890.[1] It may also explain why some developing countries don't have antitrust authorities yet. Given the limited capacity of the legal system of these countries, courts must focus on cases with a higher net benefit.

One way to keep adjudication costs under control was to work with strict rules rather than vague standards. This explains why early antitrust law heavily relied on per se rules. In recent decades, as the U.S. became wealthier and antitrust law moved from rules to standards, more and more per se rules have been replaced by "rules of reason". A similar, though less pronounced evolution can be observed in the EU.

Even now, the legal system (and the FTC) only has capacity to go after the largest players. Microsoft, Google, and Apple have to fear antitrust law, not your local plumber or sprinkler company, even if they engage in anticompetitive behavior in their small local market.

---

[1] Occasionally, rules against usury, price gauging, and the just price doctrine may have had an antitrust effect, but they were not deliberately designed for this purpose.

PART IV

Conclusion

33. Is American law the best law?

American law is likely the best law on the planet. This is not because American lawyers are intrinsically more talented than lawyers of other countries, or because American lawmakers systematically do a better job at choosing legal rules. It is the culmination of three factors that bear on the quality of the legal system.

The main factor is that the U.S. is the largest wealthy country in the world. For starters, the wealth of a country is correlated to how much it can spend on justice. Remember the "old law is cheap law" idea: the wealthier a country is, the better its law can be. The U.S. is a wealthy country, so it can afford to spend a lot to develop its legal system.

The U.S. is not only wealthy if we look at GDP per capita. It is also a country with over 300 million citizens. Those two factors combined mean that large sums in absolute terms can be spent on developing the legal system.

For comparison, Denmark is wealthy as well, but it has only 5.7 million inhabitants, which corresponds to 2% of the inhabitants of the U.S. This means that, all things equal, Denmark can spend only 2% of what the U.S. spends on judges, attorneys, prosecutors, and law professors. In other words, the U.S. is the law production factory with the largest budget on the planet. This means that the degree of legal development is higher than any other country in the world.

When I lived in Belgium, a country slightly larger than Denmark (with 11 million citizens), I regularly experienced that I had a legal question and found no answer in Belgian law books. Then I looked in the huge amounts of American literature and I found 10 cases and four law review articles about it. To put it differently, if law is like a library, then the U.S. has by far the largest legal library. No country comes even close.

The third factor is the American legal culture. Legal realism, as we have seen, means talking about the underlying problems that the law tries to solve. Because of legal realism, law review articles allow for an open discussion on optimal law. As a result, the U.S. has a larger error-correcting mechanism.

A final factor is that the U.S. is an immigrant country. It has learned more from other legal systems than any other country.

Of course, the country with the most advanced legal system is also the place where problems are seen first. For instance, the development of medical malpractice has led to an insurance crisis at certain times in the U.S.

Moreover, the U.S. does not *always* have expensive law. If the U.S. does certain procedures on the cheap, the results are not pleasant. For instance, one study found that Missouri public defenders spend on average only 8.7 hours on serious felonies—or six times less than a defense lawyer should spend (Joy, 2015).

Overall, however, the U.S. has the best developed legal system. It is no coincidence that every year, so many talented international students come to the U.S. to study law.

Index